Barefoot Days

*Events from the life
of a young country kid*

Remembered by
Glen Natalier

Published in Australia by Glen Natalier

First published in Australia 2024
This edition published 2024
Copyright © Glen Natalier 2024
Cover design, typesetting: WorkingType (www.workingtype.com.au)

The right of Glen Natalier to be identified as the
Author of the Work has been asserted in accordance with the
Copyright, Designs and Patents Act 1988.

All rights reserved. No part of this publication may be reproduced, stored in a retrieval system, or transmitted, in any form or by any means without the prior written permission of the publisher, nor be otherwise circulated in any form of binding or cover other than that in which it is published and without a similar condition being imposed on the subsequent purchaser.

ISBN: 978-1-7637888-1-7

ABOUT THE AUTHOR

Glen Natalier was born into a closely knit rural community in the Lockyer Valley in Queensland, Australia. He chose not to stay on the family farm but completed the necessary studies to become a high school teacher of geography and German language. During these teaching years he wrote a number of geography text books directed towards the syllabus requirements at that time. This allowed him to travel widely collecting, first hand, material and photographs to be used in the books. Years of teaching have left him with a love of learning and he finds that writing helps detract from the cares and worries which always seem to arise.

The tennis and footballs of previous years have morphed into golf balls which bring great pleasure when seen against the green of the centre of a fairway.

Now retired, he lives with his wife, Jill. They live in a town just over a few hills from where he was born. Their four children and their families are scattered around Australia.

OTHER TITLES BY THE AUTHOR

For my grandchildren; Jason, Lucy, Nellie, Jonathan, Sam, Lily, Luke and their grandmother, Jill (my dear wife).

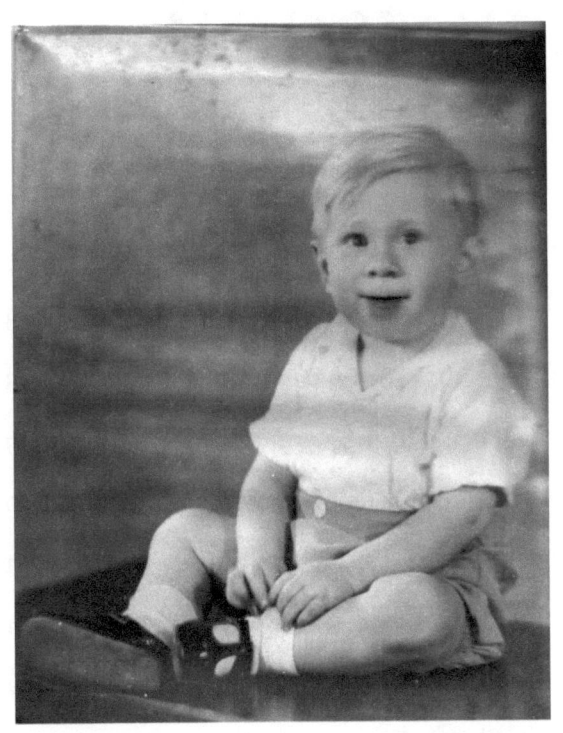

CONTENTS

1. Hello World — 1
2. A Sore Tummy — 13
3. Kelly's Boar — 26
4. Sus Domesticus — 38
5. Learning to Read — 48
6. Writing Right — 59
7. Dinner at Uncle Frank's — 70
8. Church at Ten O'clock — 81
9. Old Blacky — 91
10. A Child's Christmas I — 104
11. A Child's Christmas II — 112

12.	Hop... Two, Three	121
13.	Where there's smoke...	131
14.	Birds' Eggs	143
15.	Terry	156
16.	In the Onion Patch	166
17.	Milking Time	174
18.	The Creek	185
19.	Bringing in the Hay	194
20.	Tennis Anyone?	200
21.	D.I.Y.	209
22.	Break-up Day	217

AN INTRODUCTORY WORD

Hello.

I want to thank you for reading this book. Well, I hope you will read it after you pick it up, take a look at it and say, 'What is this?'

No doubt, if you happen to be one of my grandchildren, you are saying, 'Why, that's Grandad! That's who Glen Natalier is.'

But who am/was I really? That's probably not so important. It is for me, but as far as this small childhood memoir is concerned, I could have been any of the many young kids in the Lockyer Valley in the middle of last (i.e. the twentieth) century. Although I did write the following short pieces based on my memory of some of the experiences I had as a boy growing up on a mixed farm there, it is not so much autobiographical as generic-biographical.

Most who grew up then (there are some still around although we are becoming fewer with every edition of the local paper) could relate personally to these childhood experiences at home, at school and at church. They were **our** experiences; other kids as well as mine.

Perhaps you are now suggesting that this is a small piece of social history?

Yes, you could say that and who am I to disagree.

Who indeed?

Me. Well, I was born on the twentieth of March, the third and last son of Mr and Mrs ... But I am getting ahead of myself. That will come later.

I have not been voted into parliament to be blighted by personal ambition and political power only to neglect the needs of my constituents.

I have not been numbered with the business leaders of our country (or state, or shire, or even village) who have become rich by the sweat of someone else's brow.

Nor have I led a team of sportspeople, proudly wearing the green and gold (or any other colour for that matter), onto a grassy arena.

A celeb or an A-lister?

No, all of these have eluded me and the political decisions, the economic insights, sporting achievements, shallow thoughts or whatever, have been left for others (or their ghost-writers) to express.

I wish simply that what follows might:

Bring a slight smile to your lips.

Have you marvel that life can be so simple and so stress free.

Encourage you (if you are old enough and have the time) to remember as I have done, shake your head, and smile at your own childhood experiences.

Lucky beggar!

✶

1

Hello World

MOONLIGHT FLOODED THE VALLEY.

God's in his heaven –
All's right with the world.

Who knows? Robert Browning's Pippa really may have been passing the varnished push-up windows of the hospital in Gatton that night; they were most likely made of silky oak. It was one of those evenings when nature's beauty breathed peace and calm. Unfortunately, very few people were able to appreciate this because the town was asleep. Pippa's brief visit would have been unnoticed as well. It was, however, a beautiful, event-filled evening for one expectant mother and a family-in-waiting.

On this very night – also unnoticed but for a few – Matron Curran, with Dr Geraghty's nod of approval, was able to declare to my mother, 'It's a boy!'

Those were the days – and I am speaking about days long

past – when it was possible to know the sex of one's baby only after it had been born. A quick glance in the right direction would have told Matron Curran the answer to the question that had been foremost in my mother's (and indeed the whole family's) mind for the last many months: What's it going to be?

On the other hand, she may not have been terribly worried whether she would bring forth a son or a daughter. Just so long as 'it' would hurry up and come! After carrying the developing child through the heat of late summer she surely was relieved that her bundle of joy had finally arrived. Knowing my mother as I did, I'm sure she would have been content with whatever the good Lord had predetermined she should be blessed with.

The 'it' was me and I was a boy.

You may be thinking: *What did people have their money on?* or *Is that what Mum was expecting?* I don't know. As for what Mum was hoping for. Probably that's not really a relevant question. I have never heard my mother make comments either for or against one or the other. She did take me home, so I suppose she was happy enough with God's gift of a son.

It was indeed common knowledge some months before (six, seven, eight?) that Aggie, as everyone called my mum, was expecting. But what? Well, probably a boy or a girl. Those were the only two options available back then. It was basically a 50/50 chance for either. But apparently that's not quite true. No, I am not introducing a third sex into this story. Statisticians tell us that here in Australia there are slightly more than 105 boys born for every 100 females. So statistically it was more likely that I would be a boy. And who am I to challenge statistics? That's the thing about being born, I didn't have any say in the matter.

1 Hello World

I must admit that quite often throughout my life I have argued against this 50/50 idea. Take tossing a coin, for example. The statisticians tell us that – barring the twenty-cent coin adhering to the ceiling or sticking upright in the mud on a footy field – it will land either heads or tails. Can't argue with that. Toss a coin enough times and one discovers that half the outcomes are heads and half are tails. Fair enough. Now I ask you to think about this situation: If I have just tossed seven tails in a row, isn't my chance of throwing a head next better than 50/50?

I know what most of you will say. It would be something like this: The next throw is an independent event and both heads and tails have an equal chance of turning up. But I suggest that it is not an independent event. It is part of an event which began with the previous seven throws, and you must factor this into your thinking, into your equations, your extrapolations or whatever.

But why use tossing a coin before a football match to illustrate a theory. Take my Aunty Annie as an actual human example. She had seven boys in a row. Would her chances of having a girl next be 50/50? Or take my other Aunty Annie. She had six sons in a row. Surely the chance of her having a daughter next would be better than 50/50. Statisticians would say there was only an even chance. I would say the possibility of having a girl would be higher. So, in real life, what happened?

Unfortunately, we are left wondering; neither aunt had another child!

But I divert. As a bub such thoughts about being wanted or not wanted, whether I was male or female, would have been the least of my worries. From reports it seems that while in the cradle I had few, if any, worries. I just happily accepted my regular feeds, my dirty nappies and what life, and my brothers and sister, threw at me with a gurgle and a few kicks of my chubby legs.

Later in life I did hear that a few people suggested to Mum that it would have been nice if I had been a girl, for then she would have had two boys and two girls – sort of a double pigeon pair. Nice and neat! Now I am not quite sure when that was said, if it ever was, or by whom. How could there be people suggesting that I be a girl? It may have been when I had grown up a little and there were other factors, other than sexual symmetry, influencing their opinions.

It happened at golf recently when I was having less than memorable rounds. Playing partners have been known to say to me, 'What's wrong with you? You're playing like an old woman.' Now I know it is a bit naughty (chauvinistic? sexist?) saying things like that. But I merely smile and return with, 'What's wrong with playing like an old woman?' as I nonchalantly sink a four-metre putt.

As it was, I was delivered into a family of three. There was one girl, aged four (almost five and that would have been very important to her!) to dote and fuss over me and treat me like another one of her dolls. The two older boys, aged eight and nine, would probably have ignored me, seeing me as an irrelevance in their lives. After all, who wants a little baby brother at that age?

So, we are agreed that Mum was expecting either a girl or a boy, but the key question was: What was Mum **hoping** for? Now that's something completely different. Let's just say,

1 Hello World

because we really do not know the answer, an easy birth of a healthy child.

There, on that clear, moon-lit night, in the small cottage hospital, Willcannia (or Willcarnia, for there seems to be some confusion around its spelling), in Gatton, I said my first 'Hello' to the world. To be honest it wasn't 'Hello' but rather a startled, 'hey-watch-what-you're-doing' cry as Dr Geraghty gave me an unexpected smack on the backside. *Ouch*, I thought, *if this is what the world has to offer, it may have been preferable to stay where I was, bunched up and all!*

There is no doubt that I was born. As my biro, which is advertising a Marion Hotel, writes this on the back of used sheets of A4 paper, I have in front of me my birth certificate which verifies that fact. I can rest assured that the details listed on the certificate are authentic and true for Mr Innes, the District Registrar, who has signed the document, 'certifies that the above (i.e. the listed details surrounding my birth) is a true copy of an entry in a Register of Births in the District Registry in Ipswich.'

You see, as soon as possible after my birth (as was the case with everyone's) someone had to register the happy occurrence with a Government Department which likes to know what its citizens are up to. Being a law-abiding citizen, my dad registered me as quickly as he could, for I was such a bonnie little fellow that he didn't want anyone else to claim me. Bonnie? you query. Well, they did call me Glen; Glen Reginal to cite both my Christian names.

Yes, Glen Reginald was my parent's final decision. I have lived with it all my life. These names were certainly not chosen to highlight my proud German heritage. But therein, perhaps, lies some of the thinking behind this choice.

My paternal grandparents migrated from Germany at the end of the nineteenth century (arrived here, well in Brisbane, on 30th of January, 1888 to be exact), and those on my mother's side a little earlier. Friedrich Natalier and his wife, Maria, gave their children genuine German names as one would expect – Franz, Anna, Edi, Emma, Heinrich. With the arrival of the first World War, things German in the British Empire became less liked, so these names were anglicized (in general usage, not legally) to ease relationships somewhat. Franz was now called Frank, Anna became Annie and my dad, Heinrich, was known as Henry.

Then when the children of the third generation came along and anti-German sentiment was still widespread, heightened even more by World War II, very English sounding names were in vogue. So, with Terry and Ron as brothers, Merle as a sister and Roy, Alan, Graham, John, Mervyn and Reg as cousins, never was there a finer group of true British names sitting down to dinner with Heinrich und Franz (Oops! Sorry! Henry and Frank) and their wives Aggie and Annie.

That may explain, you are no doubt thinking, why I wasn't called Wilhelm or Gottlieb, but why Glen? That's a good question. The short answer: I don't know.

Nowhere else in our extended family does that name occur. I am not aware of any friends of the family at that time who were called Glen. I know no one within my age bracket with a name similar to mine. And no celebrities. A one off, you might say. Just a solid British name with Celtic origins, meaning valley.

And Reginald? Yes, this also appears solidly English, but maybe here we can detect my parent's camouflaged nod to my heritage. Reginald seems to have come, via Latin and French, from the old German, *Raginald*. This means 'King' I might add but will not labour the point. So here there seems to be a touch of the Teutonic.

But forgetting all the surmising, maybe these were names which Mum (Oh, and Father) just liked. They were the ones listed on the registration papers, which meant I was stuck with them.

As it transpired, already by the 6th of April – a little over two weeks after my physical entry into this world – I had become a statistical entry into the records of the State of Queensland, destined to be shuffled hither and thither, forward and backward by petty bureaucrats. But on the other hand, I had become me. Well, I had arrived and had been registered. Becoming me is something I've been working on ever since.

And those details which my dad registered with the appropriate authorities in Ipswich immediately after my birth have been with me throughout my life. I still use them to indicate who I am. On every form which crosses my path I am required to fill in my name: family name (it used to be surname); then given names (they used to be Christian names); and my date of birth (DOB) written in this format, --/--/----.

Oh! Branded for life.

'Tis outrageous, says he, to brand youngsters like me.

I also have in front of me another certificate. This one is a Certificate of Baptism. I must admit that in this whole matter of registering, so as to obtain certificates, my dad had his priorities straight. Whereas I was registered with the State

Department of Births, Deaths and Marriages on the sixth of April, he had me registered in God's *Book of Life* already on the third of April, three whole days prior. He did all this while milking cows night and morning and planting potatoes and onions and goodness knows what else.

In other words, I was baptized on Sunday, 3rd of April at the ten o'clock service in the local church. Pastor Koehler's loud voice (no microphones at that time in our church) sounded out clearly for all to hear, throughout the Immanuel Lutheran Church at Ropeley, Queensland:

Almighty and Eternal God, we pray Thee, extend Thy goodness and mercy unto this child, and receive it, according to Thy word and promise: ask, and it shall be given you; knock, and it shall be opened unto you, that it may obtain the everlasting blessing of this heavenly washing, and come to the eternal kingdom, which Thou hast prepared, through Jesus Christ our Lord – Amen.

Then as Aunty Olga, one of my sponsors, held me over the baptismal font, Pastor Koehler said, 'I baptize thee in the name of the Father, and of the Son, and of the Holy Ghost – Amen', as he thrice sprinkled water on my head. Uncle August, my other sponsor, stood to the side quietly watching. Indeed, the whole congregation was watching and paying attention. There was a particularly good turnup that Sunday for another little fellow, called Kevin, was also baptized.

Yes, I remember it very clearly as if it were yesterday. No, that's not exactly true. I don't recall it at all, for I was too young. Remember, I was only two weeks old, and that certainly wasn't yesterday. But the details of it happening are clearly listed on the certificate before me. I'm sure God remembers it.

This part of the ceremony completed, Aunty Olga delivered me back to my mother who was sitting in an adjacent pew watching attentively. Uncle Augie surreptitiously placed an amount of cash (an offering) on the baptismal font, as was the custom. It may not have been a pair of doves or a lamb without blemish, but it was a visible recognition, or token of thanks, for what God had done, and would continue to do, for me.

Mum then took me up to the altar to receive a special blessing from Pastor Koehler, both for herself and for me.

The church and the font are still there. Of the members of that particular baptism party (and of Kevin's too, I believe) I alone am left to remember.

Had I become famous a whole plethora of myths would have grown up around my birth. I could sit and dream, imagining what some of those might have been. But that's all they would be – idle speculation. As it turned out, there have been no myths, no fame.

For a long time, earlier on in my life, I did think that Easter depended on me. I was no stranger in our local church and was well acquainted with the Christian Church festivals. Easter to me, and Christmas as well, were church festivals rather than merely a time for holidays and excess purchases.

Even as a little fellow I was aware that the date for Easter varied from year to year. Easter Sunday, I knew, was always the first Sunday after the first full moon after my birthday. Taking this to its logical conclusion it was clear that Easter depended on me.

I soon was also aware that there was a full moon (well

almost) when I was born. Mum told me that the moon was very bright when Father drove her into the hospital to collect me. And if I did something really silly my sister and brothers would tell me that I was a lunatic because I was born under a full moon. The moon and I seemed to be intimately related.

Only later did I realise that it was the March equinox that was the determining date for Easter. It was purely coincidence that I had been born on that date. As for lunatics being born under a full moon? Well . . .

This all had the making of some very fine myths, but none materialized. Maybe I could still set the wheels in motion!

Neither, to my knowledge, have stories surrounding my birth and early days been passed down in our family. Mind you, there may have been a few such stories, but they have been kept from me, perhaps because they were very unflattering. I have, however, heard rumours and snippets about the following:

* Most were very intrigued when they first saw me. They felt that I had a very simian look, especially around the eyes and forehead. This feeling had never been expressed to my mother for obvious reasons. But the fact that more than one commented on it gave cause for alarm.
* It was rumoured that the doctor had to slap me on the backside several times before he could get me to cry. How many? No one was ever specific. Some said three. Some said even more. But who was there to know? Mum certainly never mentioned it. And surely one can trust a doctor of medicine and a nurse (matron indeed) not to be too violent towards a newly-born

babe. People then, and since, have tied this fictitious episode to stubbornness on my part. Surely that is a subjective judgement.

* Another story going around was that my poor mother was in labour for so long that she was starting to regret ever wanting another child. It is a fact that I was her last child. There are so many ways of interpreting this: everything from 'This is as good as it gets' to 'I never want another one like that!' Friends have frequently assured me that the consensus seems to favour the first of these feelings.
* It has reached me that an uncharitable person may have described mine as all-the-better-to-hear-you-with ears. I would have her know that they are still in fine working order even at my advanced age. No, I refuse to listen to rubbish talk like that. I shall keep my sharp hearing for processing better utterances!
* What did I really look like at birth? That's something we shall never know. Probably very similar to most other new-born bundles of joy. But simian features! Indeed!

The earliest extant photo of me is a portrait (OK, just a photo) of me when I was about two years old. It shows an alert, engaging young fellow – this being my description – finely dressed, even wearing shoes and socks. Clearly Mum had dressed me in my Sunday best for the occasion. Another photo that has survived is of us four children, all in our Sunday best. Clearly there had been a family day at the photographers.

I was the youngest of the family as you would have gathered from what I said previously. I still am. As I sit here, word-processing this, I am shocked that the youngest can be, and feel, so old.

An interesting note: I am the youngest son of my father, who also was the youngest son in his family. His father (my grandfather) was also the youngest son. My grandson, Luke, who is the youngest son of my youngest son, loves to relate that he is the youngest son of the youngest son of the youngest son of the youngest son of the youngest son of August Natalier (his great, great, great grandfather).

2.

A Sore Tummy

'I DON'T WANT ANY more grapes. I want to go back home.'

'What? We've just got here. You've hardly eaten any. What's up with you?'

'I'm not feeling so good. I've got a pain in my tummy and I want to go home.'

Sis was annoyed with me. 'Why on earth did you come crawling all this way up here with me when you had a pain in your gut?'

'I like grapes,' I replied, 'and ours aren't ripe yet. And it wasn't so bad when we left home.'

'I don't know . . .' she mumbled and then stopped. I never did find out what she didn't know.

Our neighbour Bill W. had a small orchard in the hills behind his house and it bordered our property. Apart from the various fruit trees, he had a couple of rows – short rows – of grape vines. He didn't mind if we helped ourselves to a good feed of his juicy muscatels when we felt like it. 'Plenty vor efely vun,' he would say.

It was a different situation, I might add, with his persimmon tree; with the fruit on his one and only persimmon tree. Woe betide anyone – i.e. probably mainly me and my mate Clem from up the road – he thought might be nicking some of his ripe persimmons. We would, in all likelihood, end up with his walking stick across our backsides; dusting our pants off, he called it. That would only happen if he was able to catch us unawares and we were close enough to him and his threatening mobility aid.

Expressed in mathematical terms that would be $d<ws$ where d is distance (the dangerous distance) and ws is . . . I'll let you work that out.

Luckily, we were young and pretty agile, and he had a lot of years behind him, as well as one limpy leg under him.

'Yust vait venn I catch yous, yous bloody bengels,' he would shout waving his old hand-made stick. 'Venn I see ya vaters, he vill be told.'

As we were running away, we could imagine the scene later in the day. There was Onkel Bill, as all of us young kids would call him, even though he wasn't our uncle, talking to my father over the fence or along the road somewhere.

'Vell, Heinrich,' he would be saying, 'how is eferyting goin mit du unt Aggie?' He would always call my father Heinrich even though everyone else in the district called him Henry. It is a fact, however, that Father was christened Heinrich forty years previously and Onkel Bill – he would probably have preferred Onkel Wilhelm – could see no good reason why it should be changed to Henry, world wars or not. Their conversation would continue, discussing various topical issues but not a word about how Clem and I might be pinching some

2. A Sore Tummy

of his ripe persimmons. He would not dob us in.

That was the thing about our neighbour. He was really an old softie and would just pretend to be an angry man to scare us young kids. Well, that's what we thought. Maybe we would remember him in a different light if ever he was able to physically catch us and give our pants a good dusting. His kids, and he had quite a tribe of them, were always well behaved. Which makes one think.

But back to the grape vines.

I finally did convince my sister that I had a pain, a bad pain, in my stomach and a short time later we arrived back home from our aborted feast of sweet, juicy grapes.

Mum was surprised to see us. 'Why on earth did you go crawling all that way up to Bill's grapes when you had a pain in your stomach?' Mum didn't seem terribly sympathetic either. Echoes of Sis here!

'Well, Sis said that she was going up to Onkel Bill's vines and I like grapes too, you know.'

'You should have thought!'

With the chastising out of the way, Mum got down to business. 'So now, where is it sore?' she asked, appearing a little more concerned. After all, that's how mums should be.

'Everywhere.'

'Here, let me see. Come and lie down on the couch. Does that hurt?' as she gave my belly button a poke.

'Auch! Yes.'

'What about here?' and she pressed a little lower and more to the side.

'Not as bad there,' I replied recovering from her first jab. Perhaps she hadn't poked so vigorously this time.

'And here?' as she prodded the other side.

'Auch! Oh, stop! It's real bad there. Hurts like buggery,' I reacted as the pain seemed to invade my whole lower self.

'Oh, dear me. And don't talk like that,' said Mum as she frowned, not so much at me and my language, but rather at what she was thinking. 'Did it really hurt so much?'

'Y...y-es,' I stuttered, almost in tears (maybe I really was in tears but don't want to admit it).

'Merle,' called Mum, 'do you know where Father is?' Most of us called my sister Sis but Mum insisted on calling her Merle, which was fair enough, for that was what they had christened her. Maybe it was Mum who thought of that name back then and felt obliged to keep calling her that.

Which raises another thing about my mother. She always called her husband, i.e. my dad, Father. Now there is no doubt that he was **my** father and indeed Sis' father, but certainly not Mother's father. That was Grandfather. Now, had she asked of Merle, *Do you know where **your** father is?* that would have made more sense, but she would never bother about including the possessive pronoun, **your**, when speaking to us about our father.

Clearly, she would not call our father by his Christian name either, in front of us children. Mind you, there are probably children today who do call their parents by their Christian names (*given names* official forms now call them), but that was completely off limits for us kids in those days. What she called my father in private, I do not really know, for I was never present at those times when they were by themselves. I do have a funny feeling that she still called him Father, even then.

2. A Sore Tummy

Sis, a.k.a. Merle, had strolled into the room to see what Mum wanted with her. Judging by her nonchalant entry she had not heard the whole question Mum had called out to her.

'Yes, what do you want? I was in the middle of doing something.'

'Do you know where Father is?'

'Father? No. What do you want him for?' Sis wanted to know.

'He should be home from the farm by now. See if he's down in the horse yard unharnessing the horses.'

'Yes, he probably is, but what do you want him for?' she insisted on knowing.

'It's about Glen here. I think we should take him to the doctor. His stomach really is very sore, and he seems to be quite sick.'

'He's probably just putting it on.' Sis didn't seem very sympathetic at that stage.

'Just go and find Father and tell him to hurry back here.' Mum was in no mood to argue or spend time giving explanations.

'And you hurry up too,' I pleaded between pain spasms which I exaggerated a little perhaps, but which had the desired effect of getting my sister moving.

Father must have heard some urgency in Merle's message when he received it for in a few minutes, although it seemed much longer, he came rushing into the living room. He hadn't even stopped to take off his blucher boots, which was most unusual. Father would never dare come into the house with his blucher boots on. He would always sit down on the side steps – always on the same step – and deliberately take off his working boots and socks. He would shake out each sock, make sure it was not inside out, and place it on the appropriate boot. Then he would come inside, barefooted, except in winter. When it was cold, he would keep his slippers handy near the steps and wear them inside.

On this occasion Merle must have alarmed him with her message for he walked straight into the house. Mum also must have had concern for my condition for although I saw her looking down at his feet, blucher boots and all, with a slight frown, she made no comment.

'So, what's up, Mum?' Father wanted to know. That's something else about my father that you, dear readers, have just spotted. That's right! He called his wife, Mum. This name calling was not a one-sided affair. Both Mum and Father were guilty of calling each other Father or Mum.

'It looks like the boy's quite sick. A bad stomach pain and he feels hot,' Mum explained, putting her hand on my forehead.

'What can we do? Do you think we should take him into town to see Dr Geraghty?'

'Yes, that would be the best thing to do, for he seems to be getting worse.'

'How are you feeling, Son?' Father turned to me.

'I feel like spewing.'

'Well, don't start spewing in here. I would only have to clean it up,' said a sympathetic sister.

'No, you are right. We'll take him straight into town. The doctor should know what's wrong and what to do about it.' Father was not one to hum and hah about, making the immediate decision.

'I hope it's not appendicitis,' said Mum. 'If it is, we will

2. A Sore Tummy

have to take him up to Toowoomba. The hospital in Gatton wouldn't be able to operate on him if it were necessary.'

Half an hour later, Father was knocking on the front door of Dr Geraghty's house.

Dr Geraghty? Yes, he's the one who supervised my entry into the world a few years previously. Known me all my life, you might say.

Father was knocking on the front door of his private home for it was past surgery hours. The door was soon opened by the doctor's wife.

'Sorry to bother you, Mrs Geraghty, but can we see the doctor? Our boy seems very sick.' Father got straight to the point. He was not one to waste time on small talk in any situation, let alone this one which was urgent.

'Yes, I'll call him,' and Mrs Geraghty went back inside the house quite unconcerned that her afternoon had been disturbed.

The doctor appeared almost immediately, clearly not in his surgery clothes but appearing relaxed, freed from making medical decisions. Small town doctors at that time were used to being summoned at all hours of the day. Farmers thought nothing at being up all night attending the difficult birth of a foal or calf and assumed, without a second thought, that the local doctor would have a similar attitude towards sick patients who turned up on his doorstep after surgery hours.

'Mr Natalier, what seems to be the problem?'

'It's Glen . . .' and then Mum took over and explained my symptoms to him.

'Oh, dear, I don't like the sound of that. Bring him up into the surgery and I'll examine him there.'

After being lifted onto the examination table (I was a little fellow still. Five, I think and with my sore tummy couldn't climb up by myself) the doctor began his examination. He went straight to my stomach and began pressing gently, something he probably learnt in medical school, rather than poking like Mum had done. She hadn't been to medical school. Then there was a reading of the thermometre which I was trying desperately to keep under my tongue as instructed, a few humms and haas, and a slight pause with a frown from the doctor.

It didn't take long for Dr Geraghty to make an assessment. 'I'm almost positive that he has appendicitis. And judging by his raised temperature and the pain he seems to be in, it does seem quite critical. We need to get him up to the hospital in Toowoomba as soon as possible. I'll call the ambulance. That would be the best way of getting him there.'

'But he can't go up by himself.' Mum seemed worried.

'No, one of you will have to go up with him. That will have to be you, Mrs Natalier. Your husband will have to drive up tomorrow to fetch you.' Most mums didn't drive in those days.

Dr Geraghty was soon giving instructions to the ambulance driver. 'Eddie, the boy's very sick. Get him up to the Toowoomba General as quickly as you can.'

'I'll do my best, Doc.'

'Here, I've written down a few notes for you to give them. But make sure they look at him as soon as you arrive. In the meantime, I'll give the hospital a ring suggesting that they might have to operate immediately after you get there.'

During all this organizing I was in a tight foetal position on the doctor's examining table, crying with pain and regretting

2. A Sore Tummy

that I had ever gone up to Onkel Bill's grape vines. I thought at that time that the few grapes I had eaten was causing my agony. It was a far cry from the dull ache I had in the guts before we went up there so what else could it be?

Ambulance man, Eddie, seemed the right man for the job. 'Sure, Doc, leave it to me.'

In no time, with me lying in the back of his vehicle and Mum sitting beside me, he had us heading up the highway to Toowoomba. Back then Toowoomba was situated at the top of the range some twenty-odd miles from Gatton. It is still there at the top of the range, has spread out considerably, but now is thirty-six kilometres from Gatton.

All going well, the ambulance should have reached the hospital in half an hour, perhaps a little more. But all did not go well.

I am not referring to the road which was very bumpy in parts causing my painful tummy to react even more painfully. Nor the slow climb up the range which used to cause most vehicles to labour, some even to boil, necessitating a stop to give the engines time to cool down, and have the radiator topped up with water. No, there were other dark demons on the prowl that evening, determined to inflict further pain on me.

At the beginning we were happily making good time. Well, Eddie was happy enough, chatting with my mother whom he knew from way back. Mum was somewhat apprehensive of the whole situation, and I was moaning in agony. The volume of the moans rose and fell depending on the size of the bumps in the road, which more often than not he failed to avoid. In all fairness, perhaps he really did evade more than I thought.

Just past the hamlet of Grantham, Eddie's mood took a change. It was there he was later heard to relate that, in automotive parlance, the shit hit the fan.

'What the . . . ? What's that up ahead there?'

'Don't say there's been an accident.' There was concern in Mum's voice.

'Hard to say from here, but there seems to be a lot of headlights stuck up there not doing anything.'

'They do seem to be moving, don't they? Perhaps not very quickly though.'

'Oh, no! It couldn't be!' blurted out Eddie.

'What? What do you remember?' asked Mum, becoming more concerned.

'A convoy of Yankee army vehicles, a long one, went through town earlier this afternoon. (Historical note: This was during war time – World War II war time – when there were thousands of American servicemen scattered throughout South-east Queensland and there were always some of them moving around). But they should be much further on than here. Shit, I hope they are not causing some sort of a hold-up. But I suppose we will find out sooner or later.'

2. A Sore Tummy

And we did find out, as soon as we reached the last of the banked-up vehicles. Word had travelled down the line that there was a problem in Helidon. Something about the bridge over the creek there being blocked.

Eddie took matters into his own hands. He put the flashing light on and moved off driving on the wrong side of the road.

'Shouldn't worry the Yanks too much,' he observed to my mother while giving a little chuckle, 'They would be used to seeing vehicles driving on the wrong side of the road. And it's only a couple of miles to Helidon.'

'But what if we meet a car coming towards us?'

'Well, there doesn't seem to be any traffic coming this way. And if anyone does decide to come towards me, he will just have to get out of my way.'

His progress was brought to a halt at the Criterion Hotel in the middle of the small town of Helidon. The road in front of the hotel was a swaying mass of American servicemen, all holding glasses or bottles of beer, singing, talking, shouting.

'Good God!' said Eddie. 'The old Criterion has never had business like this before.'

'That might be good for the pub. And for those soldiers too, but what about poor Glen?'

'Right, I'll see what the hold-up is all about and what can be done about it.' He jumped out of the ambulance leaving the lights flashing and pushed his way to the entrance of the hotel. It wasn't long before he returned shaking his head and smiling.

'I got onto an officer in the pub who promised to see what he could do. But only after I told him I had a dying child and his frantic mother in the ambulance who had to get to the hospital immediately.'

'Oh!' cried Mother. 'Dying? What did Dr Geraghty tell you? Is it so bad?'

'No, don't worry Aggie. I had to tell him something to get him moving. There has been an accident on the bridge ahead. You know the bridge, that low one just down there around the corner. He will come and help and see if we can squeeze the ambulance through.'

'We won't all end up in the creek, will we?'

'No worries,' replied a confident Eddie.

We did squeeze past the trouble on the bridge. A couple of American vehicles had collided. They were probably not on the wrong side of the road. We didn't tip over the side of the bridge into the Lockyer Creek below. Which was just as well because there had been quite a bit of rain in the past weeks and the creek was running pretty full. And our effort did bring a cheer from the soldiers who were working to clear the crashed vehicles from the bridge.

None of this eased my pain but it was a relief that we were on our way again, up to the hospital where they could do something about my worsening condition.

'Where have you been? We've been expecting you for the past hour.'

'Bloody army convoy stuck in an accident over the creek at Helidon.' Eddie gave a clinical assessment of the reason for his taking so long in delivering his patient.

The doctor looked at me squirming on the hospital trolley.

'Oh, dear!' he exclaimed as they rushed me into the operating theatre.

2. A Sore Tummy

Note 1. Some of the details in this account may not be quite accurate for I was in severe pain which could have affected my memory; but who is around to question my accuracy?

Note 2. I survived the operation (I had to have two, actually – the first for acute appendicitis the second for peritonitis resulting from a burst appendix) and, from time to time ever since I have had a reoccurrence of that excruciating pain to remind me of my good fortune.

Good fortune? Where was the good fortune in all of that? You may ask.

Clear. Getting to the hospital before I died. And it is a fact that since then I have never really enjoyed eating grapes, although Onkel Bill's muscatels cannot really be blamed for my attack of appendicitis.

3.

Kelly's Boar

I GREW UP ON a mixed farm. Well, I did until I was old enough to be sent off to boarding school. Sent off? That seems a little harsh. It sounds as though my parents just couldn't wait to pack my bags and be rid of me. Let me assure you that nothing could be further from the truth. They were sorry to see me go and always happy to have me back during the holidays, helping around the farm, for there was always plenty to do. I sometimes had the feeling that they would save up jobs, especially for me to do during my time at home.

A mixed farm? Yes, there was a little bit of a lot of things happening there. Father, with the help of us kids, and mum, grew a whole range of vegetable crops for sale and milked some cows. These provided cream for the local butter factory and skimmed milk (that is the milk which had the cream separated out of it) for the pigs which were raised to be sent off to market.

An agro-economist might talk today about product diversification or multiple income streams. Father could be more hands on, perhaps more earthy, in his descriptions: 'A man gets a good crop of spuds but so does everyone else in the valley and you can't sell the bloody things. At least the cream cheque comes in every month.' Or again: 'Spend months feeding the blighters and get bugger-all for them at the pig markets. Let's hope the onions do well.' That's putting it in real farming terms – lose on one, win on the other (hopefully).

So, Father did not have to depend on one source of income like the monoculture agro-businesses of today. I don't remember ever starving as a child so this widely practised approach to farming must have worked. I do remember often running into the kitchen after getting home from school and crying out, 'I'm starving to death, Mum. Any cake left?' But it seems I've survived. And there were always plenty of jobs waiting to be done – in the cow bails and pig pens, down on the cultivated land or up the hill somewhere. Mum's 'We will miss you when you go off to college' probably had a double meaning.

Father was born to be on the land and yes, he was passionate about his jack-of-all-trades farming. It was his life. The income generated by the farm, as a result of our hard work, was sufficient to adequately care for our family. I learnt enough (chipping onions in a cold westerly wind) and experienced sufficient (milking cows on a frosty morning) before I left for boarding school to make me less passionate about farming and as time went on, I realised I had more interest in education than in agriculture.

We milked the cows, separated the cream which was sent off to the local butter factory and then fed the separated milk to the pigs. Father always kept two or three breeding sows, each of which – when her fullness of time had come – would deliver a litter of fine piglets. Ten, twelve or even more; one couldn't know until they were actually born and rooting around in the straw looking for a teat to latch on to. Occasionally, very occasionally (to be honest it was only once), I was allowed to be present at the birth of a litter. It was an exciting experience for me and probably a great relief for mother pig.

'Eight . . . nine . . .'

'That's ten, not nine. You missed one.' My older brother disagreed with me. He did on many other occasions too.

'No, I didn't!'

'You must have.'

'Now shut up for a while. You've made me lose count. How many do you make it, Father?'

'I think there's thirteen and that's probably all there'll be.'

'How can you tell?'

'You can see how the old girl is so relaxed now and almost smiling.'

The number was always a spirited topic for discussion around the tea table the next evening after the final tally was confirmed. Here was an income stream waiting to grow up, and it didn't take a mathematical genius to work out that the greater the number of piglets, the higher the potential income.

These little chaps would be looked after, first by mother pig and then later by father with the conscripted help of his three sons (that's me and my two brothers). They would be cared for, well fed and fattened until they were ready to be taken to the saleyards in Gatton. Pig sales were held there every Thursday. On our farm, as was the situation on all farms in the district, it was a case of these little piggies would go to market.

3. Kelly's Boar

They must be given credit for contributing to the income of the mixed farm and to the welfare of our family. As well as drinking the separated milk every morning and evening, they were also fed the unsaleable products grown on the farm – wormy potatoes, spotty pumpkins, weevilly corn. And also, I might emphasise, Swede turnips which were grown especially for them. They didn't live solely on leftovers. These little fellows would grow up to become porkers or fat pigs. They were an important component of our mixed farming economy.

The two or three sows were permanent residents on the farm, but father had no boar, and a boar was necessary in the breeding process.

His problem was solved by Uncle Otto, our neighbour, who lived just a little bit further up the hill. He did own a boar, a big, black brute with a broad, white saddle over the front of his back running down both front legs. He was a brand of pig known as a saddleback. Father's sows were not saddlebacks, but this posed no problem for this old fellow. He was no racist. At the appropriate time, and father seemed to know when this was, he would ask Kelly (everyone in the district called him Kelly for some reason) for a loan of the boar.

Uncle Otto (a.k.a. Kelly, and he was indeed my uncle; great uncle really, for he was my mother's uncle) would agree to walk the beast down the hill to our place. Now some boars can be contrary old buggers, dangerous indeed, but this fellow, called Kelly's Boar if my memory serves me correctly, was quite tame and could easily be directed along the road by a switch in Uncle Otto's hand.

On this late morning which I want to refer to, he probably started off a little hesitantly and even reluctantly, not wanting to be separated from his lay-about habits and familiar mud-hole in his home sty. After a hundred or so uncertain yards (Kelly's Boar didn't know about metres) during which the guiding switch would regularly be used, his whole attitude changed for he realised he was out on the open road which felt OK. He was out of the close confines of his pen.

Uncle Otto would never try to bring old Kelly's Boar down by himself. This procession of two, were it ever to eventuate, would be something to behold. Leading would be a grossly overweight, underworked pig, being followed by a rotund, old farmer whose speedy days were well behind him. These two were so well suited to one another that it would take something quite extraordinary to cause either of them to break into a trot. The slow would be leading the slower. Or the other way round. It was hard to know which. Such a procession would be seen as a dirge in slow motion.

True, he was aware that the animal could get away from him if he had a mind to and it would not be good to have a boar, wild or not, roaming free about the district. But that was unlikely to happen. No, Uncle Otto would not be out alone with his boar on the public by-ways for he would inevitably be accompanied by his dog, a blue cattle dog whose name was Bluey. The dog would be there invited or not, for he would follow his master wherever he might go. Most often the outings with Uncle Otto were unexciting – a walk down the paddock to see if the gap was tightly closed; maybe down to the windmill to see if the water level in the tank was correct; maybe walking around one of the grazing paddocks looking for thistles or burrs to chip out.

This trip, however, promised to be a little more exciting, for the dog would have something to herd, something to chase, and this is what he was bred to do. A cattle dog is an active creature. When nothing seemed to be happening around his place and boredom was setting in, he would start herding Aunty Annie's chooks. They were generally compliant, soon all ending up under the barn. His efforts at rounding up the pigeons were never successful. They would all quickly fly away when one of them spied the dog coming, only to return when Bluey lay down again.

Today he could hardly keep still. It mattered little to Bluey that this was a pig and not a cow. There may not be any sinewy hind legs to nip and get his teeth into but there was a pair of inviting pig's trotters. Every few minutes he would dart in and give poor old Kelly's Boar a nip which wasn't really appreciated by either pig or master.

Uncle Otto lost patience after a few unwarranted forays by the dog.

'Get behind, you stupid bugger. Leave the pig alone!'

With each nipping the annoyed pig would turn around and snort a couple of times, probably expressing the same sentiment as Uncle Otto. Dog would at first take little notice. After all he was bred to do this (well, perhaps not to pigs exactly) and the odd word of discouragement was certainly not enough to override his pedigree.

Nip. Nip.

'Snort. Snort.'

'Stop it, I said,' shouted Uncle Otto, 'or you'll get a good kick in the arse.'

Nip. Nip.

'Snort. Snort.'

'I won't tell you again. Leave the pig alone or you really will get that kick.'

It was unlikely that Uncle Otto would carry through with his threat. No, not because he was so fond of the dog – although he was but would not admit it – and did not want to mistreat him. Nor was it because he was gentle in nature and it would grieve him to physically punish any creature. My mate, Clem, his son, would bear witness to the fact that his dad could deliver quite a sobering smack on the backside. The real reason was that the last time he tried to give the dog a kick he missed because the dog was too quick and evasive. Uncle Otto fell flat on his backside, hurt himself and had to slowly limp home, there to face his family with embarrassment and a bruised gluteus maximus.

For the blue cattle dog, nipping the boar did not have the same excitement and thrill of adventure as herding cows. Rounding up the cattle was a battle of wits, a continual battle to see who was the boss. Nip one of them, and the dog would see this as a point for him, but the reaction from the assaulted beast was likely to be immediate and potentially lethal. Well, perhaps not lethal, but certainly painful if one of the kicking legs were to catch an unaware or slowly reacting dog in the face, or anywhere for that matter. There would be a whelping and whimpering and Bluey would retreat to lick his wounds and recover before continuing his life's mission. Just another round to the cow.

Even more humbling would be having to bear the tirade of abuse coming from his master when a lucky kick did find its mark.

'You sleepy mongrel! Don't you ever learn?'

'Old Puss would do a better job than you, you dumb duck!'

Oh, how humiliating to be rated so low among the farm animals. The blue cattle dog should be king!

'You're supposed to be a cattle dog, you stupid bugger! Don't you have ears?'

But all these comments would be offered with a loving heart and the dog would receive a friendly pat when he came running back to Uncle Otto with his tail between his legs.

Today, however, there is the slow, rather mundane, unexciting task of herding the old boar. He almost wished he was still at home dozing in the shade under the pepperina tree gnawing on one of his bones or perhaps having another go at the pigeons.

But a job is a job, his dog-brain thought, *and I will probably get the opportunity for a snarl and a sniff at old Bluey next door when we finally get there.* (Yes, our dog was also called Bluey. If the truth be known most of the blue cattle dogs in the valley were called Bluey.) *Perhaps we could race off up the hill together and flush out a hare or two. One day I'm going to get one of those long-legged rodents!*

The trek continued.

At the bottom of the hill Uncle Otto flicked the boar's nose with his long switch and directed him through our front gate which was usually open. Suddenly his blue dog raced on ahead.

'Come back here, you damned mongrel. Where the hell do you think you're going?'

His dog took no notice.

'Bluey. Bluey. Heel! Come back here you deaf bugger!'

There was no reaction from the dog. He kept running up the track to our house barking his lungs out.

Disturbed from napping under mum's special poinciana

tree our dog, called Bluey as Kelly's Bluey well knew, was racing down to meet him, barking even more loudly.

Upset by all this duo of barking the old boar had awakened from his slow, even walk and broken into a trot. He veered off the track and headed off cross-country with Uncle Otto puffing after him.

'Where the hell are you going to, you silly old coot?'

On hearing something hot on his heels, Kelly's Boar changed tempo but not direction. He was now racing towards our dam, which just happened to be full of water for a change. He did not stop but plunged straight in. Luckily at that point where he entered the dam, the water deepened only slowly, and the pig was able to avoid drowning and to stand submerged up to his rump steaks.

And there he stood looking at Uncle Otto who didn't know whether to swear at the pig who had evaded him, at the dog who had upset him or just swear at life in general. What could he do? He was in his normal working gear of long work pants and blucher boots. He was reluctant to go into the water, sink down to his hips and get everything wet. Taking his boots and pants off was definitely not an option. He did have his pride and never did wear underpants.

Uncle Otto just stood there looking at the pig who was looking at him. Both were wondering what to do.

At this stage an appropriate phrase/statement comes to mind. I most certainly came across it for the first time in the Grade VI Reader at primary school. It comes from a short story in a book called *The Relief of Lucknow*. The British forces are facing inevitable defeat by the native Indian Sepoys who had recently revolted against British control. The wife of a

3. Kelly's Boar

British soldier (Scottish probably) is lying semi-conscious on the floor when she suddenly shouts, 'Dinna ye hear it? Dinna ye hear it? The Campbells are coming.'

She had heard the pipes and drums of an advancing column of Scottish soldiers coming to relieve the town. I have no Scottish blood in my veins but ever since grade six that phrase, 'The Campbells are coming', pops into my head whenever some sort of relief is at hand. Actually, a friend of my wife, Donald, did play the bagpipes at our wedding, but even that did not put Scotch in my veins.

Back to the pig in the dam, or more accurately, to the sunroom in our house just up the hill from the dam drama. Father had been awakened from his short after-dinner nap. The dinner-time nap was part of the schedule on a mixed farm. Well, it was on father's farm. He would finish his solid mid-day meal eaten to the accompaniment of the market report and the hill-billy half hour on the local radio station, 4GR, and then lie down on the couch for half an hour.

'What is that racket all about? If it's not those bloody Yankee planes waking me up and frightening the chooks, it's something else.'

Now father was usually a very mild-mannered man, not one given to very bad language. He was not alone in this. I think I wouldn't be far wrong in suggesting that this applied to almost everyone living in the district. Most were regular worshippers at the local church where the Pastor would urge – and that quite frequently – his congregation members to flee 'bad' language. Occasionally, however, when he was particularly annoyed or passionate about something a 'bloody' might slip into father's expressions.

'It's the dog barking,' was my helpful reply.

'I know it's a dog barking. Sounds like a whole bloody pack of them. What are they all barking at?'

'I don't know,' was my innocent reply, for I didn't know.

'Well, go and have a look.'

'Maybe someone's coming,' I suggested.

'Well get out of that comic book and go and see who it is, can't you?'

At that stage I decided, rightly, that our discussion was over, and I went out to see what was causing our dog to be so upset. It wasn't long before I returned.

'It's the dog from next door,' I explained to father.

'What? Otto's dog? What's it doing here?'

'Oh, and another thing. It's quite funny really. Well, I think it's funny. Uncle Otto is down beside the dam shouting at his boar who is in the dam.'

'What?'

'Uncle Otto is down near our dam and his boar is in the dam,' I repeated.

'Yes, I heard you. What on earth is... Oh! That's right. Otto said he would bring his boar down this afternoon.'

'This should be fun,' I said, 'watching Uncle Otto getting his boar out of the dam.'

'No smart comments, OK? Come on we will go down and help him get the old fellow up to the pig house.'

Once we had quietened the dogs down, Kelly's Boar was quite content to continue his excursion up to pig yards. Very soon with his curly tail twitching and a smile on his snout he realised where he was actually heading; and why. He broke into a trot and his low-hung bag of masculinity began swinging excitedly from side to side. Once at our pig pens, he was guided up a ramp into the pig house where his inamorata – at least for the next few days or so – was awaiting him.

Yes, I was the one who had to go into the dam to chase that stupid old animal out. I came out wet up to the top of my pants. And to top it all off, mum went mad at me for getting my pants so wet and smelly.

'Heavens above, boy, you smell like a pigsty. Where on earth have you been?'

4.

Sus Domesticus
(Pigs to non-Latin speakers)

CLEM AND I WERE in the shade under the big pepperina tree up near the pig pens. We had our shanghais and were trying to knock over a few sparrows. As I remember we were not having much success and were sitting on a couple of sandstone blocks lying under the tree, deciding whether we should stay there any longer or go over to the forest to see if there were any new nests being built in the tall ironbark trees there. The blocks were left over from a number father had dug out from a small stone quarry at the back of our hill. He had used the others to build a low retaining wall in one of the pig pens as well as along the bottom side of the tennis court.

We were sitting there waiting for the sparrows to return. Our first few shots had missed their targets and frightened the birds away, but not for long. The tree was their hangout place, a sort of sparrow settlement, and they had built a number of nests there. Most of the nests were within reach of our climbing abilities but we would leave them alone for we had a good selection of sparrow eggs in our collections and would not go robbing the nests just to smash the eggs. We knew from experience that in a little while they would all come back and give us a chance to have a few more shots.

We used to call them bird brains and said that they didn't know they were in mortal danger with us around. My big brother, Ronnie, would laugh and say that the sparrows knew they were safe with us firing at them and that we were the bird brains for thinking that we could hit any of them with our shanghais. This seemed a rather cruel criticism of our accuracy because both of us considered ourselves to be pretty good shots. To be fair it was a high tree, and the birds had a nasty habit of sitting near the top. And another thing. As you all know, sparrows are quite small birds and if you were to take their feathers away there is hardly anything left to hit. This called for 100% accuracy which was something hard to achieve with the jaggy little pebbles we were using for ammunition.

My sister, Merle, was also keen to put her tuppence ha'penny worth in when we were talking about shooting sparrows with our shanghais.

'It says in the Bible that two sparrows are sold for a penny.'

'If you say so, but what has that got to do with us trying to shoot them?'

'Just wait till I go on.'

'Well? We're waiting.'

'It also says that not one of them will fall to the ground without God's OK.'

'What does that mean?'

'It's clear. It's up to God whether you hit or miss.'

'Ah. Get away with you. You'll be spouting the fifth commandment at us soon.'

The birds had not yet returned, and we were watching a tall man wearing a wide-brim straw hat and well-worn blucher boots approaching. He also had on a flannelette shirt and long working trousers. We knew who it was. It certainly was not Santa Claus in disguise. We looked at each other a little concerned.

'What are you two scallywags up to?'

'Just trying to shoot a few sparrows, Father.'

'As long as it's just sparrows.' Father did not like us shooting at anything but sparrows, crows and pigeons, all of which he considered pests.

'That's all. Fair dinkum. You know there's no crows or pigeons in the tree here to shoot at.'

'And what about the doves and red beaks which are here?'

'No, we wouldn't shoot at them. You know that.'

Which was often true, and with father around, always and definitely true. We didn't relish being given 'a good kick up the backside' with those blucher boots, which he always wore, for shooting at protected (by Father) species.

'Well instead of just sitting around here doing nothing why don't you go and chop up half a dozen of those big, old pumpkins lying up there near the shed to boil up for the pigs?'

We realised that this was not a question. Father seemed to have missed the point that we were not 'just sitting around' but actively engaged in ridding the farm of some avian pests. Even being of a tender age, we were old and experienced enough to know that when father suggested we do something, it was best to do it. We took a quick look up to the top of the tree to see if our targets had returned so that we might have a final shot at them. But no sign of them. Our hunting was over for the time being and the sparrows lived to frustrate us another day. With Father standing and watching that we were taking up his suggestion, we hung our shanghais around our necks, emptied the stone ammunition from our pockets and went to the pig food shed. We located the tomahawk and started chopping up the pumpkins. Halfway through our assigned lot we were interrupted.

'Howdy there, young fellows. That's some mighty fine hogs you got yourself here.' This comment came from one of the two American soldiers who had turned up and were watching what we were doing.

American soldiers? What were they doing on our farm?

A little knowledge of world and local history will give an answer. During World War II, and I'm talking here after the United States joined the war (i.e. after the Japanese attack on Pearl Harbour in December 1941) hundreds of thousands of American troops passed through Queensland on their way to fight the enemy in the western Pacific region. Many of these soldiers spent time in, and around Brisbane.

The whole countryside was dotted with temporary army camps housing the soldiers awaiting further orders. One company had spent some time – weeks? months? I don't remember how long – camping in one of our paddocks just across from the pigsty. When I went to feed my two poddy calves which were kept in one of the pigpens I could look across and see rows and rows of khaki army tents. Yes, our farm was invaded, but the soldiers had come in peace. They were carrying out military manoeuvres up and down our hill, but there was no enemy hidden there firing bullets at them. All they seemed to be doing was frightening the wrens and finches away from their nests.

Before being shipped off to invade some enemy-occupied island in the South-west Pacific they had time to enjoy the rural peacefulness of our farm.

At this moment two homesick soldiers had been looking at our batch of fat pigs and apparently tasting pork chops.

'Yes, beauties, aren't they? Father says they are coming along very nicely. Be ready for the pig sales in a couple of weeks,' I replied putting down my tomahawk.

'What do you call them?' asked the other soldier who seemed to be interested in farm work.

'We call them pigs,' answered Clem and started giggling.

The soldiers looked at one another, apparently a little confused. They leaned over the paling fence and said something to a couple of the pigs which had come up to them. They then tickled them on the forehead (they were friendly types, our pigs, or maybe they anticipated a small gift of food) and then turned to us and said, 'Yes, we call them hogs, but I know you call them pigs, kid. We wanted to know if you have special names for them like Clara or Rosie.'

'No, that's what we call our aunties. I also have an Aunty Olga. She's my godmother,' I replied, quite happy to have stopped work. We were now talking happily to the strangers although Father had told us to keep away from those Yanks. 'They are not really pets. They don't stay with us long enough and so we don't give them special names. We do name most of our cows, but.'

'We do too,' said Clem joining the conversation. 'Do you want to know some of the names we call our cows?'

4. Sus Domesticus

'No, don't bother. You probably have names like Moo-moo or Daisy-bell. But if you are standing here talking about the pigs, how could someone know which one you are talking about?' asked one of the soldiers.

We could see the soldiers smiling at each other when they asked the question, so I replied, 'Father calls them 'this pig' and 'that pig'. But you couldn't do that.'

'Why couldn't we call them that too? Is our accent so hard for the pigs to understand?' one of the Americans wanted to know.

'Because if you called that pig over there near you 'this pig' it would get all mixed up, what with father calling her 'that pig' and you calling her 'this pig' it would be very confusing for her. She wouldn't really know whether she was this one or that one.'

'Say, kid, do you ever get a clip round the ears at school for being so cheeky?'

The soldiers were clearly enjoying talking to Clem and me. They obviously had nothing better to do and wanted to stay talking. It was Saturday morning and perhaps the soldiers did not work on the weekend if the enemy wasn't around. There weren't any enemy troops around our place, or indeed in all of Australia, but at times Father didn't seem too sure. 'Those bloody Yanks. They make so much noise, you'd swear that the Japs had landed.'

'Anyway, tell us, why are you chopping up those blue marrows?'

'They are not marrows, they're the pumpkins we grow on the farm. Father sells the good ones, but if they are too big and knobbly like these here, or have mouse holes in them, we chop them up and boil them in this big drum with sweet spuds and wormy potatoes. We feed this to our pigs.'

'Say, that sounds more appetizing than some of the chow they often serve up to us. No wonder they look so fat and juicy.'

I continued with the conversation while Clem turned away, again watching for the sparrows.

'You can see that these pumpkins are bluish in colour, so they are called Queensland blues.'

'Yeah, that makes sense.'

'Some of the farmers around here grow big orange-coloured ones especially for the pigs, but Father doesn't do that. Your dad does, doesn't he, Clem?'

'What?' Clem wasn't listening but was watching the

4. *Sus Domesticus*

sparrows returning to the pepperina tree.

'I just told these fellows that your dad grows pumpkins especially for the pigs.'

'Yes, he does. Big yellow ones.'

'Oh, and we do have a special pig as well as these,' I told our guests.

'Oh. Tell us more. What is this special hog of yours? Or should I say special pig? Do you have him here or are you hiding him somewhere else?'

'No,' I replied, 'we have him here in the pigsty. That's him down there under the gum tree in that pen. He has a special name.'

'Really? And what is his name? Is it 'this special pig' or 'that special pig'? Say, what's your mate laughing about?'

'Clem,' I said, turning to him, 'why are you laughing?'

'I don't know. I'm just laughing,' was Clem's answer. This, if you think about it, wasn't really an answer at all.

'Our special pig down there in that yard,' I said getting back to the main topic, 'is called the Christmas pig.'

'The Christmas pig?'

'Yes, Father keeps one and fattens him up. A bit before Christmas he takes him up to Toowoomba to the bacon factory there. They kill him for us and make him into different things – bacon, pork chops, roasts, a ham and pork sausages. They even send the feet and head back. Mum makes brawn out of the head and we boil up the feet in salt water to make pig's trotters.'

'The Christmas pig, hey. That fellow down there under the gum tree must sure feel lucky to be the Christmas pig. What about you, lad?' the American asked turning to Clem. 'Does your dad have a special Christmas pig?'

'Most farmers around here keep one of their porkers especially for Christmas. Ours is a black one,' replied Clem, 'with a white band over its back.'

'A black one. And what do you call him?'

'The Christmas pig. And it's not a 'him'. It's a 'her'.' Clem always liked to be correct. Well, most of the time.

'Oh, I'm sorry for mixing up the girls and boys.'

'Yes, my dad thinks they taste better than male pigs,' Clem explained. 'But don't ask me why. It's just something my dad thinks. We take her up to Toowoomba in the back of our ute when she's ready.'

The one soldier looked at his mate. 'Well, imagine that! It seems as though we have a couple of real hog experts here.'

'And then after Christmas, Father keeps the wurst pig in the same pen,' I kept the conversation going and the soldiers were happy to stay.

'Worst pig? What do you mean by worst? Is he the naughty one and doesn't get on with the others and has to be locked up by himself?'

'Not worst! Wurst. We make wurst out of him.'

'What on earth is wurst?'

'Wurst is sausage we make. Mettwurst. Don't you have that where you come from?'

'No,' they agreed, 'we've never heard of it. Tell me, what sort of sausage is this wurst of yours?'

'Well,' I started to explain, 'Uncle Harry, that's Aunty Olga's husband, fattens up a steer – you know what that is, don't you? – and Father fattens the pig. That's the one we call the wurst pig. Then when they are big enough, we slaughter them up at Uncle Harry's place. They are minced up together into sausage meat. Mum and Aunty Olga mix all sorts of herbs and stuff with the minced meat and it is squeezed out into the cleaned pigs guts. They are tied up into rings which we hang up in the garage. They are then smoked in the fire father lights there.'

'They move the car out first,' interrupted Clem.

'Uncle Harry does the same with his. Father puts plenty of sawdust on the fire so that it smokes well. That's wurst. He says that different types of sawdust make the sausage taste different.'

'So, from what you say, it's a sort of smoked sausage,' remarked the American.

'Yes, that's what I said.'

'I'll tell you something,' said one of the Americans to the other, 'I sure bet the little pigs here sit around hoping that they don't get put in that pen down there with the gum tree. Say, kids, you'd better get back to that chopping of yours or you'll end up in the stew when your dad comes back.'

'Bye for now,' said the other soldier. 'Been nice talking to you. Now we know all about pumpkins and Christmas pigs and wurst pigs. Wurst? That's how you say it, isn't it?'

'Be seein' ya, Yanks,' said Clem in his version of an American accent.

'Cheerio,' I said. 'If you want to know more about our pigs you know where to come and who to ask.'

As they walked away, they said something to each other which Clem and I couldn't quite hear. We finished chopping up the final two pumpkins before going back to the pepperina tree to have another go at the sparrows.

5.

Learning to Read

THE EARLY YEARS OF my life rolled round – let's say the first five years – and apart from nearly dying from a severe case of appendicitis, which was not brought on by eating the neighbour's grapes, I don't remember much about them. It seems I was just a happy, contented little fellow. There was no preschool or kindergarten – maybe in the cities but not out in the country where I lived – so all my early education, acquiring social skills, developing a moral and religious compass and stuff like that, took place informally. This was mainly within the family, but also at church, visiting relatives and friends and playing with neighbouring kids. Then it was time to go to school. I was six years old.

Yes, I was six years old and ready to find my place at the local primary school.

Going to school was no big deal. **Upper** Tent Hill State Primary School with its one teacher, Mr Barton, and its thirty odd pupils, was just a few miles up the valley. **Lower** Tent Hill State Primary School with its one teacher – I don't know who

5. Learning to Read

he was – and the same number of odd pupils was just a few miles down the valley. I went upstream. Had our farm been next door, I would have gone to the Lower Tent Hill School. But it wasn't, so I didn't. The road leading up to our place divided the catchment areas of the schools.

My big sister was still going to school when I started and so, theoretically, I had someone to look after me. Whether she did or not is anyone's guess, for I don't really remember. Probably not, for she was a girl, and girls tend to stick together at school and to her mind I was just a nuisance of a little brother. And really, I didn't need any help. I had been going to church and Sunday School with most of the kids at school and so it wasn't anything new or scary.

Unlike many, or most, kids today, I couldn't read before I went to school. It wasn't that I was particularly backward, and no one suggested that either. Well not seriously. At least I didn't think that they were serious. No, there was just no good reason why a young, energetic country boy like me, should be able to read before he went to school. Schools are there to rectify that.

There were plenty of other things that I had learnt to do. Milk a cow, for example. Or hit a tennis ball with a tennis racket. Oh, and also with a broom stick. If you are not familiar with the term, it is a broom handle without the sweeping part attached.

And what else? Yes, I could climb trees, walk on dry, sharp, khaki prickles (some people call them bindi-eyes today) without shoes on. When I think about it, I walked everywhere without shoes on, except for going to church on a Sunday. I had to wear shoes to church on a Sunday, and socks. That was part of getting dressed up in my Sunday best. I knew the local names for all the birds in the area, and there were quite a lot. I also knew the names of all my cousins. There were quite a lot of these too!

And sing? Yes, I could recite, and sing the words of most of the hit songs of the day. We had a big, upright radio in the dining-room which was usually switched on to a station playing music, mainly 4GR Toowoomba or 4WK Warwick. There was Bing Crosby's *I'm dreaming of a white Christmas*, Vera Lynn's *There'll be Blue Birds over the White Cliffs of Dover* and other artists, whose names I have forgotten, singing *Deep in the Heart of Texas* or *I've got Spurs that jingle, jangle, jingle*. The list goes on and on. I remember them all. Occasionally I hear an old-time record being played which contains some of those old hits and I am transported, or is **beamed** the correct word, to another age. Many a time I am tempted to sing along with these songs from times long gone.

Yes, and I say this in all modesty, I was competent in all the above and more. My early life was spent doing things and learning things. By just being a kid growing up in the country I acquired many skills, so there was no need for pre-school back then. But **read**? No, that was something that I would learn to do at school. What do they say? Yes, that's it. School is for the three Rs – reading, riting and rithmetic. If you need to learn to read, you go to school.

Father and Mun regarded reading as necessary – essential indeed – so I went to school. I started in Prep I and we got straight into this reading business. You could say that I started learning to read at the very beginning, the very beginning of the slim volume, *Queensland School Reader Preparatory I*. I've

5. Learning to Read

since checked it out again and it was on page 4 where we started our great adventure into the world of the written word. So, it was not really at the beginning. We began with the very first letter on page four. Yes, you've guessed it. It was an 'a'.

The letter was positioned beside a coloured drawing of an apple on a little branch with a few leaves. And below it was written, *'a' like an apple on a twig.* Yes, the 'a' did look like an apple. There was full agreement on that. Approached from a different point of view, you could say that the apple was purposely drawn to look like an 'a'. The book took us through the whole alphabet in this manner. First an illustrative drawing below which was a short statement tying an appropriate letter to it. I can still remember most of them. I mean the drawings. I know the whole a,b,c, from alpha to omega.

Later (you know that would be after 'e'), there was *'f' like a feather,* and a feather was drawn which indeed looked like an 'f'. *Kicks his leg up?* Yes, 'k', which I still see on TV quite often. At that time, they were not using poor old 'k' to advertise a certain type of breakfast cereal, although it did exist. Then moving right on... No, wait a minute. Moving back one letter we find a jumping fish. You guessed it! 'j'.

There are two of these illustrated letters that even to this day I use – make that **confuse** – quite regularly: 'b' and 'd'. I am a little dyslectic at times – well, that's what my wife tells me – and I often get things front to back. Sometimes my 'bs' come out looking like 'ds'. However, if I remember that *'b' is like a bat and ball,* and that *'d' drags the drum,* I avoid embarrassing typos and my dad doesn't come out as bad. My wife also says that my dyslectic tendencies get so dad at times that I have trouble with numbers such as 111, 707 and her age.

That's how I got to know my 'as', 'bs' and 'cs' at school. Not learnt in isolation but associated with some recognisable everyday objects which were drawn to look like a letter. Thinking back over these alphabet-looking illustrations, bridges come to mind, arched bridges.

I was never happy with the 'm' and 'n' and felt that 'n' should come before 'm' in the alphabet. Both 'm' and 'n' were represented by bridges, arched bridges, like the Romans used to build. In the alphabet in our reader, the letter 'm' *was like a much wider bridge* and the next letter 'n' which *was like a bridge* seemed a little out of order. It would have been more logical for 'n' to come before 'm'. Then the first mentioned, i.e. 'n' could have been like a bridge and the one following, 'm' in my revised order, like a much wider bridge.

Whatever! Maybe, at some time in the distant past grammarians mixed these two up. In the overall scheme of things why shouldn't 'n' come before 'm'? If this were the case, I would have to remember that to get an 'm' I would merely have to add one more span to the bridge at 'n'.

Ed. Note. Stari Most in Bosnia is a good example of an 'n' and Pons Fabricus across the Tiber River in Rome is a good 'm'.

Which brings to mind a photo of the Richmond River bridge in Tasmania which I took some years ago. No, it was not built by the Romans, but by convicts serving their time in that colony. These felons built the bridge there with a whole number of stone arches keeping the road from falling into the creek below and injuring or perhaps killing some of the ducks which always seem to be there. In other words, that bridge has several 'ms' and 'ns' immediately next to each other. Like some ancient Greek manuscript, it is very difficult

5. Learning to Read

to understand. There is no indication whether one should read 'double m, double n', or 'n, double m, n', or possibly some other combination. Check it out. You may have better luck at arriving at what they were trying to tell us.

But looking back I feel that I have mastered the alphabet. Yes, even my 'bs' and 'ds'. I could say that they were drilled into me, by chanting in class the whole 26 letters over and over again.

    a   like an apple on a twig
    b   like a bat and ball
    c   like a cake with a bit taken out
    d   drags the drum
    e   Oh! Dear me! What did e look like? That's right. And empty egg. A little imagination needed here.

Etc. etc.
Then came the big letters:
Big A   like an attic. What's an attic, you may ask.

Big N   like a narrow gate. You can guess what big M was like.

Big T   like a tree. The tree had to be severely pruned to have the required shape.

Etc. etc.

This chanting would not take place in the classroom proper but out on the veranda. Our one-teacher, rural primary school had only one room – a large one indeed – which had to accommodate the whole school enrolment of around 30 pupils. It would be disturbing to have half a dozen enthusiastic learners loudly chanting in the midst of those wishing for a quieter learning environment. Having proven to be trustworthy we Prep I pupils, all six of us, were allowed to sit outside with our readers in hand often waving in front of our faces to keep the flies at bay.

Out in the open air we would shout our alphabet, through and through, again and again. If I remember correctly, the two girls were always the loudest. We boys, particularly Clem and me, were much quieter. The reason, I suspect, was that we both had older sisters at home who were always telling us to 'Be quiet! Don't make so much noise. Can't you see I'm trying to listen to the wireless?'

Thinking back, it would have been quite exciting to have gone on a fieldtrip to help with learning the alphabet. This would have worked especially for those letters where the big, or capital, letters looked the same as their small brothers. Let's take 'O' and 'X' and 'S' for example. Come with me now on a short excursion.

'X' is like two crossed sticks. We would have no trouble

5. Learning to Read

finding a couple of sticks, making them the same size and crossing them. Then lay two longer sticks in the appropriate arrangement beside them and one could actually experience the difference between small and big 'x'.

'Sir,' a voice is heard, 'do you have two sticks in your book press back at school?'

Mr Barton frowns but does not reply. We boys knew what sort of stick the voice was referring to and were all grinning.

Now we'll go next door to the orange tree in Mr Barton's backyard.

'Here's a small orange which has fallen off,' begins Mr Barton and then he continues, 'Glen could you climb up the tree and pick that big one up there.'

Side by side these two pieces of fruit clearly depict the difference between big and small 'o'.

'Ray! Come down this instant. We do not need any more examples.'

Little 's' and big 's' could be a bit more elusive but I'm sure if we poked around in the long grass and rubbish on the creekbank we could find possible contenders. Getting them to form into the desired shape would be more difficult.

'There's a dead snake on the road outside our place,' offered Beryl. 'We could go and look at it. But there's only one. I'm sure it's a big 's'.'

'No, Beryl, there's no time to walk all the way up to your place just to see a dead snake. I'm sure we've all seen one already.'

As I said, there were no excursions back then, so we had to be content with learning to read inside the classroom, from a book.

The alphabet well drilled, well learnt, became implanted in our memories for life. I must admit however (and very few know this, not even my wife) that sometimes I am looking for the 'js' before 'h' in my Macquarie Concise Dictionary.

Luckily my literary education did not stop at 'z' *like a zig-zag path*.

No way! We moved right on to the capital letters beginning with *Big A is like an attic*. Big? Yes, strangely enough they were not called capitals but 'big'. Mr Barton, our teacher, must have adjudged us preppers to be quite advanced for we called them 'capitals' right from the beginning, in spite of what our reading book was telling us. Progress with these big letters moved along very smoothly and much more quickly for by now we were really into the swing of things.

After having a firm grasp on the essentials, we tacked these big letters onto a combination of small ones so that we were able to form words and then string them together to create sentences. Wow! Things were now starting to happen.

First up were the 'at' words – bat, cat, fat, Nat, mat, sat and probably some others that I have forgotten. Sentences were formed, and the stories began:

The cat sat on the mat.
Nat sat on the mat with a bat.
The cat was fat.
The cat had a hat.
Nat sat on the mat with the fat cat with a bat.

The class was excited. We could run home and show our parents that we could finally read, and we were still in prep.

5. Learning to Read

'Mum, listen. The cat had a rat on the mat.'

'What? Where? Did you chase it out? You know that the cat is not allowed to bring rats and mice inside.'

'No, Mum. We learnt that at school today.'

'Was it Mr Barton's cat?'

'In reading, Mum. We are learning to read the 'at' words. And my name is in our reading book.'

'What? Glen? That's not a 'at' word.'

'It's my nickname, actually. Nat. They call me that at school. Didn't you know that?'

'That's nice. Tell me. Did you sit on the mat with a cat or a rat?'

'You're being silly, Mum. Can I have another piece of cake?'

'No, it might make you fat.'

'Ah! I'm still hungry.'

'You will have to wait till teatime. And another thing.'

'Yes, Mum?'

'When you go outside wear your hat. The one that you sat on and made flat.'

Yes, the boy in the story, if you could call it a story, was really called Nat. I was quite thrilled about this for that was one of my nicknames. Fancy being mentioned in a book widely used in Queensland schools. Everyone would be reading about me. Natty was my other nickname. I preferred this one for 'Natty' meant neat and smart. I interpreted this as meaning clever, intelligent. Yes, that suited me, whereas a 'Nat' was some kind of bug. You spell it gnat, I was later to learn – probably when we were learning about silent letters. But when you think about it my name does begin: G. Nat . . .

Yes, the 'at' words were conquered and all wrapped up in

stories. Keep going at this rate and we would soon . . . well, be at the 'an' words – can, fan, man, tan, etc.

School propelled me into a whole new world, a world of reading, and I loved it. Still had a long way to go, to be sure, but the building blocks were lying there waiting. OK, the stories which we could read at that early stage (e.g. The fat cat sat on the mat with a rat) may seem trivial and uninteresting to some but then I am reminded of Dr Seuss and *The Cat in the Hat* and other similar titles. People seemed to have engaged with them.

We young country kids were excited to be reading those elementary sentences. The important thing, I believe, is not so much what we read but that we could, and did, read.

As we grow older, this changes. There is so much written material out there and **what** we read really does become an important consideration for each one of us. You have just read the above, but please do not judge me too harshly!

At school, after the reading, came the (w)riting. Our teacher, Mr Barton, did teach me (w)riting, too. But that's another story, on another page.

6.

Writing Right

A PEN?

Now what sort of pen might we be talking about? A pig pen? No, I didn't think so. Way back when I was in primary school. You want me to envisage some sort of pen from so long ago? That's asking a bit much, isn't it? Let me think...

Well, there's the horse paddock along the creekbank beside the school. Some people called that a pen, the horse pen. That's where kids who rode a horse to school would leave their transport during the day. However, those who really knew their way around the school, i.e. us kids, didn't call it a pen. It was a paddock. Not a big paddock I admit, but a paddock nevertheless. If it were too big, smaller kids might have trouble catching their horse when school was finished for the day. But then again, horses usually knew when school was finished, and they were keen to get home too. They would walk up to their young masters quite happy to be saddled up again.

Are you thinking about a chook pen?

Where people keep the hens?

What? You want to call it a hen pen?

Where Mrs Barton kept her hens?

Yes, we called that a pen, but a **chook** pen and not a hen pen, and that one was not in the school grounds. It was in the teacher's place next door. Which is true, but one side of this chook pen was part of the schoolyard fence. Looked at this way it is fair to say that it was part of the school.

OK. Call it part of the school if that would make you happy.

But no, I don't want to talk about a chook pen, the one at the school (almost) or any of the other ones which dotted the district, for most of the pupils at the school would have had some sort of protection for their poultry at home.

Talking about that chook pen (which, I know, you're not keen about), do you remember the time when Noel jumped over the fence, opened the gate of the pen and let all of Old Jack's hens out?

6. Writing Right

Who could forget it?

The chooks thought it was great. Freedom! They were running around everywhere in Jack's backyard, picking and scratching, chasing one another, making a devil of a noise. The gerberas and coleuses in the back garden had never had so much attention; all was unappreciated however, especially by our teacher, Jack, and his wife.

It is a wonder that Jack didn't notice them running around before he did.

He wasn't even the first to notice them. He was too busy keeping us in order. It was his wife. She came running over to the classroom to tell him. Don't you remember? That's a sight we will never forget.

Yes, that was something, wasn't it? Seeing his wife run.

And then the fun we had rounding them all up. All of us kids stamping around in their back yard. We probably did more damage to his plants and flowers than the hens would have done had they been there the whole day.

No, he was not amused.

And who dobbed Noel in?

It must have been one of the girls. One of the teacher's pets.

No, Mr Barton didn't have pets. He treated everyone the same.

And Noel got six of the best. I bet none of the girls ever got six. Call that equality?

They must have hurt too, for when he came out of the office he was not smiling as we would usually be if we only got one or two on the backside. He was ringing his hands.

Yes, I remember the stoic face Noel presented to us all who were curiously waiting near the office to see how many he would end up getting. We would have been surprised if it had been fewer than six because Mr Barton was really annoyed. A few days later, after the pain had subsided, but with the palms of his hands still a little redder than normal, Noel admitted that it was all worth it. The stern stuff of heroes could always be discerned in Noel. They bred them tough in those days, especially at the foot of the mountains.

We kept well away from the our teacher's chook pen after that.

But back to my original thought. The pen I had in mind is the one that is more powerful than the sword. What does the Good Book tell us?

They shall beat the ploughshares into inkwells
And their pruning hooks into pens.

No, it doesn't say that. It says that th*ey shall beat their swords into ploughshares and their spears into pruning hooks.* Didn't you go the Sunday School?

Well, for the present purposes I prefer my version with pens and inkwells. These are the types of pens I want you to envisage. These are the pens people used to write with (most people today would add 'in ancient times'). A pen was a simple pencil-shaped piece of wood with a steel nib at one end.

A steel nib?

Yes, the steel nib was the important part of the setup. You would dip that specially designed nib into the ink and it would hold a small amount of that ink. Its sharp, pointed end (well, fairly sharp) would gently distribute the ink onto the paper when you wrote with it. This pen would be lying with a pencil or two in the routed-out pencil holder at the top of the desk.

And it did have other uses.

What did?

The pen you are talking about.

What other uses?

Don't you remember? They were often used to stab the person sitting next to you in the backside.

Oh, is that what you mean? That was a bit naughty, wasn't it?

Yes, but only one or two cuts from Old Jack, if you were caught.

It was understood that you wouldn't yell out if you were poked with a pen. The trouble was you were often surprised and jumped and let out an 'auch'. And then the girls would not play fair and yell out just to get you into trouble.

Then if you were caught you got two if you had stabbed a girl and one if you had poked a boy with the pen nib.

That doesn't sound fair. Where's the equality in that?

I got caught a few times. Both times Beryl was annoying me, and she forced me to jab her with my pen. I ended up getting the cuts. Two each time.

You should have jabbed Des or Cecil. It wouldn't have hurt so much.

But they weren't annoying me. Why should I jab them?

It was only the older kids who were allowed to write with pen and ink, wasn't it? We younger ones were only permitted to use slate pencils and lead pencils to practice our literary and calligraphic skills.

You remember how the top of the desks contained not only

a routed groove in which to place one's writing implements – pen, pencil and slate pencil – but also a round hole in which was placed a white porcelain ink well and a slit which held the pupil's slate?

Yes, with all this writing equipment so ready to hand one was led to believe that this writing caper was a cinch. Not so! As a neophyte warming the well-polished forms behind the desks, I was not allowed to use all of it.

That was the sad reality. Some of this advanced technology was reserved for kids in the higher grades. As a result, writing with pen and ink, catching flies and drowning them in the murky waters (ink) in the ink wells was something the preppers could only look forward to.

My writing career (meant in the very general sense) began with a lead pencil and copy book. With these I learnt the art of running writing which my wife has difficulty reading today. I blame it on my left-handedness.

You write with your left hand, do you?

No. That's just the problem. I probably should, but I don't. That's another story. Let's now go back to school.

The teacher is in front of a group of eager-looking prep pupils. There were six in my intake, a bigger than normal number for my small country school. The year my friend, Peter, started school was more typical. Actually, it was the year he didn't start school. He would have been the only one in his class and as he never stopped telling everybody: 'There would have been no one to come second in the class'. To overcome this problem, he had to start a year earlier and always be the youngest in his class. That was a neat solution for there

6. Writing Right

would now be sufficient in his year for someone to win a bronze medal. There was fierce competition in my year with us six little beavers always lined up ready to go.

'Now children, take out your copybook and pencil.'

At this stage five little kids jumped out of their seats and ran towards the mechanical pencil sharpener affixed to the teacher's table out front. This was a machine, barrel-shaped, with a handle for turning its hidden inner mechanisms on one side and different sized holes (for inserting different sized pencils) on the other. Used correctly it would shape the end of a pencil into a beautifully rounded sharp point, eager to create beautiful writing.

This simple machine excited us kids for we had nothing like it at home. There, pencils would be sharpened by using one of Mum's peeling knives. This needed skill and a certain amount of care. My big sister did this at home. I only tried when my Mum wasn't around. Then I would get roused at by Sis. At least I could argue back with her; something which would earn me no points were I ever to argue with Mum.

This magic machine at school was simple to use. All you had to do was to shove the pencil in a hole on one side and turn the handle like mad on the other. But it was a hungry little machine. If you kept turning it would keep chewing up the pencil, quickly shortening it. I'm sure many parents would often wonder why their little kids at school were using up their pencils so quickly.

When Mr Barton had told us to get ready to do some writing, all of us, except shy, little Sarah, had rushed out to sharpen a pencil whether it was necessary or not. Sarah was still searching in her pencil case for a suitable weapon.

'Sir.'

'Yes, Sarah?'

'Which pencil shall I use?'

'How many do you have?'

'I have some red ones and some blue ones and a whole lot of others.'

'Let me see.'

Old Jack (he could be a sympathetic soul at times) would search through Sarah's bulging pencil case to see what he could find.

'Don't you have a plain black lead pencil, Sarah?'

'Yes, I think Mummy gave me one like that, but I can't see it here anywhere.'

Mr Barton continued flicking around in Sarah's pencil case while all the time keeping one eye on the pencil shortener on his table. Eventually he gave up.

'Why don't you use this pretty red one? You won't have to sharpen it. I'm sure you will write beautifully with it.'

'But I want to use the pencil sharpener too, Sir.'

'You might have to wait until tomorrow. Then you can take one of these blue ones out and sharpen it. I will make sure you are first in line tomorrow.'

Poor Mr Barton knew from previous experience that at the beginning the most exciting thing about learning to write was sharpening one's pencil. Now, many years since that time, I find that if I need to write something I spend as much time fiddling around, tidying my desk, looking for Thesaurus, having a cup of coffee, lining up my biros and generally planning my approach, than actually writing.

Finally, with everyone's pencil sharpened – some noticeably

shorter – copy books opened at the correct page; writing can begin.

Writing?

Tracing actually.

Our first step in conquering the second 'r' of our school days, was to practice drawing the various shapes which combine to form our English letters and subsequently our running writing – the upstrokes and downstrokes, the loops and circles, the dots and crosses.

'Sir.'

'Yes, Dessie?'

'We write across the page from our left to our right, don't we?'

'Yes.' Mr Barton was wondering what Des was getting at.

'Why?'

'Why what, Des?'

'Why do we go that way and not the other?'

'I suppose it's because our letters slope that way. It would be too hard for us to make them go the other way. Even you couldn't run backwards if you were leaning forward.'

Clem joined in the conversation (probably to get out of practicing his loops). 'They write the other way on the page in some countries, don't they, Sir?'

'Yes,' agreed Mr Barton, 'but they have different shaped letters. Now I think you better practice putting nice straight crosses on your ts.'

We all learnt our writing style from the same copy book, so all our upstrokes and downstrokes, our dots and crosses should be similar. It makes me wonder if later in life the writing style of us all should be the same. Clearly it is not.

What went wrong?

My copy-book handwriting has definitely gone downhill. I blame biros, ball-point pens. These seem to have a mind of their own. They want to go slipping all around the page rather than staying on task. The old-fashioned pen, holding the ink in readiness was happy, indeed was waiting, to be guided neatly on the page, running from one letter to the next.

I was interested to see how a more recent edition of an Education Department Copy Book has endeavoured to make this early writing exercise even more exciting for budding authors. 'Trace over the loopy pattern with your finger', the book directs pupils, 'while saying 'round and round'.' This reminds me of a verse from an old Banjo Patterson poem (Yes, all his poems are old!). It goes:

And an answer came directed in a writing unexpected,
(And I think the same was written with a thumbnail
dipped in tar).

The old shearer who wrote this must have had some fore knowledge of modern copy books.

Having mastered the loopy patterns, the modern youngsters can now move onto the 'humpy patterns'. Do they write any more beautifully, or clearly? I don't really know. The problem is one doesn't often get to see someone's writing today. Most only poke at images of letters on their smart phones or speak into their computers if they want to 'write' something.

'Didn't you learn to write before you went to school?' I was being questioned by a young, enquiring mind who could write (i.e. punch letters on a tablet) his name before he could walk.

6. Writing Right

'No. Why should I want to write before I went to school?'

'Well, you know. So that you could write.'

'But why? Who would I write to?'

'Perhaps your mum, or maybe your sister.'

'But I lived in the same house as them. Why would I want to write to them? If I wanted them to know something I would simply talk to them. I could talk before I went to school, you know.'

'Well perhaps your playmates. Or Clem up the hill. You are always talking about your mate, Clem.'

'Write to Clem? That would be pointless, for he couldn't read yet.'

'Well, I just thought . . .'

'And another thing. What would Old Jack, our teacher, have to teach us if we knew everything before we went to school?'

'Do you want a game of Scrabble, Grandad? But no funny, old-fashioned words.'

7.

Dinner at Uncle Frank's

Come, Lord Jesus, be our guest,
and let these gifts to us be blessed. Amen.

AT AROUND TWELVE O'CLOCK on a Sunday, as indeed at each mealtime on every day of the week, this simple prayer of thanksgiving could be heard rising from the district's farmsteads, finding its way to ever attentive divine ears. My Uncle Frank's home was no exception. As a child – he would have been my Onkel Franz then – he had learnt to sit at the table and wait patiently until his father – my grandfather – offered a prayer of thanksgiving for the meal about to be eaten. It was the same prayer Uncle Frank now offered, except back then it would have been said in his father's native German language:

Komm Herr Jesus, sei unser Gast
und segne, was du uns bescheret hast. Amen.

7. Dinner at Uncle Frank's

Now he also insisted that his family (and all guests who had joined them at the dinner table) wait until he had said grace.

We (my family and I) had come to share Sunday dinner with Uncle Frank and his family. We had been to church in the morning (well, most of us had) and now both families were standing around talking, waiting for lunch to be served. When Aunty Annie working in the kitchen with son Roy, one of my cousins who was helping her, saw that everything was ready they called out for everyone to take a seat. There was a little shuffling and shifting about until all those anxiously waiting were seated.

'Who else is there to come?' asked my father when he noticed that one set place was still unoccupied.

'That's Mervyn's. He's still trying to wash the grease off himself. He's spent all the morning tinkering with that new bike of his,' replied Aunty Annie.

'What! Is he AWOL again?'

'No,' replied Uncle Frank, 'it's legitimate leave this time; it is leave for the weekend. They've given him a job in Brisbane teaching officers how to ride. He likes telling officers what to do.'

The whole district knew of my cousin Mervyn's on-going fight with the army. He was Frank and Annie's oldest son, a tall, strapping, healthy young man and the only one of the family to be called up to do compulsory military service during World War II. But he was shy and as he put it 'reluctant to shoot at people he did not know in a war he did not start.' For twelve months he had played hide and seek with military police. When first drafted he was being sent to Townsville, 1800 kilometres from his farm, for basic training but he jumped train before arriving there and three weeks later turned up back at his home. Then began a cat and mouse game during which Mervyn would clear off up the mountains when word reached him that the military police were on their way up the valley.

This could not go on indefinitely and finally when it was realised that Mervyn was an expert bike rider and mechanic he was given a job in Brisbane training army riders. With this, all were contented and so he spent his army days well away from enemy danger. 'But not from danger,' he was always quick to add when talking about his role in the war. 'It's pretty damn dangerous teaching those drongo officers how to ride a bike. They're likely to run you down if you don't watch out.'

In a short while Mervyn appeared, and lunch could begin. As he sat down, Merle, the only daughter in both the families, when she saw the hands beside her fiddling with the cutlery, felt it her duty to kick her little brother, that's me, under the table and say, 'Wait until Uncle Frank says grace.'

'What did you kick me for, Sis? I was only straightening my pudding spoon.'

'Well, you should have your hands folded waiting for grace rather than playing with your spoons.'

'I didn't see your hands folded!' I got in the last dig.

Once table grace was completed, we were all free to enjoy the Sunday roast dinner set before us on plates brimming full.

Already on coming through the back kitchen door we had become aware that there would be roast duck for dinner. Those brown, crackling aromas seeping from the front door of the Crown wood stove were easily recognizable. But even before then, most of us would have anticipated roast duck for dinner.

7. Dinner at Uncle Frank's

The majority of farmsteads in the district had a poultry flock in which the hens provided eggs and ducks the Sunday roast dinner. We also had some guinea fowl and bantams and occasionally some turkeys. The turkeys we would eat when they were ready, but the guinea fowl and bantams would just run around and provide some colour and variation in the flock. 'Useless damn things', my father would comment when they had upset him in some way. This was especially the case with the guinea fowls who could be very noisy at times and disturb his lunch time nap.

Aunty Annie also had a number of geese but today duck was on the table. The crisp-skinned flesh and a slice of richly spiced stuffing (I had been given a leg) would be liberally surrounded by a variety of vegetables all grown in the home garden or as part of the farm's production – potatoes, pumpkins, beans and carrots, perhaps cabbage. And to top it all off there was a covering of rich onion gravy.

The full flavour of the meal won by the toil of the farmers and prepared by the hand of grateful family members joined with the simple prayer of these people and rose on high as a fragrant offering of thanksgiving for the blessings bestowed on those who worked the soil.

'Hey, Aunty Annie, did you cook the gizzards?'

'Well, Glen, yes and no,' Anna replied (Aunty Annie had originally been christened Anna but no one called her that anymore. Perhaps Uncle Frank did in private).

'I don't understand you. Did you, or didn't you?'

'I didn't cook them separately, but I minced them up with other bits and pieces and put that in the stuffing.'

'Oh, that's a pity. I like the gizzards,' I went on, a little disappointed.

'Glen don't be such a pill,' butted in my sister who was always on the lookout for occasions when she might comment on my behaviour and try to pull me back into line. She must have seen herself as my guardian, my moral policewoman. 'You don't like gizzards at all. You never eat them at home even when Mum does give them to you. Here, do you want the parson's nose instead. Aunty Annie has given me one of them. You never want that at home either.'

'Yes I do. I like the parson's nose, but only when it's nice and crispy. Sis, do you know that eating the parson's nose will make you run faster? If you eat enough of them, you might even be able to catch me when you're chasing me.'

'Don't be ridiculous. Where did you get a silly idea like that from?'

'Well try and see, why don't you. You might win a race with me by a nose.'

I remember the dinner around the large table as a happy, friendly affair. Frank and Annie's large dining table had to be extended by the addition of a table normally kept on the veranda. With this extension, all fourteen members of our two families could sit together, albeit a little crowded.

With their six strapping boys who were always hungry,

7. Dinner at Uncle Frank's

and me and my two brothers (who were also always hungry) Annie was worried that the two large ducks might not satisfy all the hungry mouths. With piles of vegetables filling each plate they managed to accomplish their task with just a little room left in each stomach. This was just as well (or planned) for there was more to come. Heaven forbid that a country meal should stop after duck and vegetables.

'Hey, what's for pudding, Roy?' I asked after I and most others were nearing the end of the first course. I had not quite finished everything on my plate but was already looking forward to something sweet. I directed the question to Roy for I knew that during the week he spent a lot of time in the kitchen helping his mother feed the other six men in his family.

'Well, young fellow, why don't you just wait and see.'

'Oh, come on. I bet it's bread pudding and boiled rice. Mum says that you are the expert at making bread pudding. Hey, Sis, did you see what pudding we were having?'

'No, I did not,' answered my sister, 'and if you don't finish your cabbage and pumpkin, you mightn't be getting any.'

Conversation kept bouncing around the table as the meal was enjoyed. Both sets of parents occupied one end of the table and they were happy to talk among themselves. For the boys it was a free-for-all. How are the cabbages coming on? How are you getting on with that girl next door, Alan? Who was that redhead I saw you talking with in Gatton at last week's cattle sales? How's the new bike going? Did you go to the pictures last night? Who won the tennis between you and College View? The topics brought up were of work, of entertainment, family matters, friendships and leisure. These were questions that portrayed the daily life of young farming lads in the district. I was still too young to be involved but my time would come. In actual fact, it didn't, for I had chosen a different path. I had other interests at that time as well, interests which the older boys had already grown out of, and mostly I would just sit and listen.

Finally, the time had come. Perhaps not quickly enough for those keen on a good plate of pudding; but it had come.

Merle and I got up from our places and went into the kitchen ostensibly to help hand the plates around, but really to quickly satisfy our curiosity as to what would be served up. We joined Roy and his brother Reg who, while listening to the radio from which Bing Crosby was crooning *I'll be Seeing You*, were doing the serving out.

'Angel's food! Did you make that, Roy?'

'No, Merle,' he replied, 'that's Mum's specialty.'

'And green jelly,' I shouted as I watched Reg get a large dish of shivering green out of the fridge.

'And,' continued Reg, 'that's not all. There's custard, and I'll open a couple of bottles of preserved pears that Mum did last year. That will be two fewer bottles we have to eat our way through. The tree was loaded last year and Mum did a number of batches. We've been eating preserved pears ever since.'

'I'm sure I still have room for a few pieces and they will get rid of that taste of cabbage,' I said as I used my finger to wipe up a splotch of spilt custard on the kitchen table and put it in my mouth.

'Here, take these plates out to Mum and Father and make yourself useful,' said Merle, now that Roy and Reg had finished filling the fourteen bowls.

7. Dinner at Uncle Frank's

This was the nature of a Sunday lunch here and I remember having more than just one. It was always a happy occasion. And none of the lunches would have been complete without a liberal portion of dessert, often with the boys going back for second helpings. In this household storing the leftovers was never a problem.

The dessert spoons clattering into empty plates indicated that hunger had been satisfied. A short prayer of thanks was recited by Uncle Frank and the large gathering soon dispersed.

Frank and Annie's house was a typical Queenslander – a weatherboard house with wide verandas on two or three sides set on high stumps. One veranda would normally face north to catch the winter sun and it was this spot with its couch and squatter's chairs where Uncle Frank and my dad ended up after lunch. They made themselves comfortable in the chairs, pulled out their tobacco tins which held a plug of tobacco and a pocketknife and cut off a filling for their pipes.

After a little sucking and puffing the two men were soon enveloped in a haze of differing aromas. My dad was the first to comment. 'That plug of yours has rather a nice smell. Do you know what brand it is? Don't know that I've come across it before.'

Frank thought for a while as he took a few more puffs. 'Yes, I like it. Only been using it for a few weeks. I think it's called *Old English*. The barber sells it. He put me onto it while I was having a haircut. That would have been at the last pig sales.'

'Yes, it's good out here in the open but it might be a bit strong-smelling for me if I were to smoke it all the time. I like my *Edgeworth Mild*, so I'll stick to that.'

A comfortable silence reigned as the two brothers rested in

the winter sun after their filling Sunday dinner. Small puffs of smoke continued to rise from the two pipes. This was a scene of complete contentment. Soon both heads drooped and tired hands rested the pipes on the arms of the chairs.

'What the devil?' My dad's nap was interrupted by a loud motorbike that went roaring up the hill in front of the veranda. 'Who are those two maniacs on that bike?'

Whereas the two older men of the families were content to sit and quietly have a pipe and chat on the veranda in the sun, the sons had more active pursuits in mind after dinner was finished. Roy chose to help the women clean up after the meal, but all the others headed outside. Alan was seen heading off across the creek towards the neighbour's house. Uncle Frank's two youngest boys were keen to show off their new air-rifles which they had recently purchased. So these two, together with Ron and me, went to the storeroom under the house where they kept them.

'Shall we go up to the big fig tree and see if we can get a few sparrows?' suggested Ron, who prided himself on being a good shot.

'I don't think we'd better do that,' said Graham. 'If Dad hears about it, we'd all get a good kick up the backside.'

'What? Even for shooting a few sparrows? They're only pests.'

'Yes,' came in John, my other cousin, 'the Boss has made it very clear that we are not to shoot birds of any kind.'

'That's strange. You'd think he'd be happy for you to get rid of a few of the sparrows.'

'And some of the pigeons too,' I put in. 'Your hayshed is full of them.'

7. Dinner at Uncle Frank's

'Nope,' said Graham, 'that's his orders.'

'What can we do then?' went on Ron. 'We just can't stand here looking at these two things. We want to see if they shoot straight.'

'Well,' suggested John, 'first we'll get a few empty jam tins out of our dump and go behind the shed for some target practice. Then we can go over to the barn and see if we can get a few rats. He doesn't mind us shooting the rats.'

While we four (I wasn't really helping and they only just tolerated my presence for I was too young for them) were organizing the afternoon's shooting entertainment, the older cousins made straight for the work-shed where Mervyn kept his latest prize possession. He had always had a great interest in motorcycles and he had just taken possession of his latest, a second-hand BSA.

'Feast your eyes on that!' he said to his younger cousin, Terry, as he opened the door. Terry, my oldest brother, had recently bought a motorcycle too and appreciated what he saw. Whereas he was duly impressed he would not consider it appropriate to show his feelings.

'A BSA. You know what that stands for don't you?' he asked Mervyn.

'Of course. It's named after the Birmingham Small Arms Company that manufactures them. Everyone knows that. What are you getting at?'

'Well, I've heard it stands for Bloody Sore Arse.' And he laughed.

'Get away with you. You're just jealous for you know that your Triumph comes nowhere near this little beauty.'

The admiring and discussing continued until Terry made

a suggestion that Mervyn knew would be coming. 'Let's go for a spin and see what it's worth.'

A few minutes later with Merv opening the throttle and Terry riding pillion they were roaring up the road in front of the house causing distress to their fathers on the veranda.

Later in the afternoon the family members came drifting back to the house. It went without saying that midday dinner at someone's place also included afternoon tea at around 3 o'clock. The fruits of a Saturday morning baking in the kitchen would now appear on the dining table. The mass-produced products of Arnott's and Webster's would be shunned in favour of freshly baked cakes, slices and biscuits. Why spend money buying biscuits when you can make your own? Indeed, it was a point of honour for Aunty Annie and Roy that there would be a suitable selection of offerings for the visitors. Oh, the shame if a visitor should arrive to find the biscuit tins empty.

Now armed with a huge pot of tea (no instant coffee in those days), and decked with sponge rolls, chocolate cake, ginger slices, jam drops and not forgetting a large slab of streusel kuchen – another one of Aunty Annie's specialties – the table was ready to fill the imagined holes in our stomachs. When Roy called everyone in for afternoon tea, he did not have to call very loudly or for too long.

Once afternoon tea was over, it was time for us to go home because the cows would be waiting there, as they were here too at Uncle Franks. Milking time had arrived.

Life on a mixed farm was not just roast duck and pudding.

Church at Ten O'clock

MINE WAS A CHURCH-GOING family within a church-going community. The Sabbath (Sunday to us) was there for going to church. The essential jobs on the farm such as milking the cows, feeding the pigs and other animals were attended to but all else could, nay! **had to** wait till Monday. Sunday was a day of rest and of going to church.

Most people in the district went to the Ropeley Lutheran Church. Sure, a few went to the small Baptist church down the road from us beside the creek, or the one at Rockside, but these were the only two other churches in the area. Oh, yes, that's right. There was a small church next to Uncle Harry's place. But what denomination? I don't remember. It's not there anymore. The few, and I mean very few, Anglicans and Catholics who lived nearby had to go further afield. The odd person went nowhere. Most in the valley at that time when I was a kid were evangelical – German Baptist or Lutheran.

Around where I lived at Upper Tent Hill were farms owned by – and I'll list them in geographic order, as I remember

– Weier, Pieper, Dodt, Dodt, Steinhardt, Steinhardt, Zeiser, Bernoth, Krenske, Krenske, Natalier (that's me) Weier, Garmeister (then there was the local pub; not owned by a German name but certainly patronized by many), Jackwitz, Tillach, Reiman, Bachmann, Steinhardt, Steinhardt, Logan, Logan. Logan (what happened here?), Grams, Natalier (that's Uncle Frank's family), Grams, Grams. You get the idea?

And that was just in our little valley. I could do the same for the Ropeley Valley over the hills to the east, with different names of course, but all were of German origin; and for those who lived in those hills between.

And they were all regular church goers, members of the Ropeley Lutheran Church. Well, fairly regular. 'I wonder where Alf is today?' It just would not do to hear statements like this too often. Much better to turn up every Sunday and not have people talking about you. Mind you, it was also seen as the weekly social outing. For most, it was the total social life.

8. Church at Ten O'clock

Factor in the large families which were common, and the result was a large, thriving congregation with its large church (the church is still there) out in the countryside at Ropeley. There it stood alone with only the cows and corn crops to keep it company; except on Sundays.

The babies kept on coming and the congregation kept on growing. My mum left school at quite a young age, as was normal for girls at that time. She worked as live-in help for pregnant and new mothers of the congregation. She was never out of work!

Church here was at ten o'clock. The time was fixed in cement. Probably it was arrived at to fit in with the farm work schedule which included milking the cows, feeding the calves and pigs and then cleaning up to have breakfast. There wasn't time to start anything else (and this was, after all, Sunday, a day of rest) so may as well get ready for church.

'Glen, have you got your shoes on?'

'Yes, Mum.'

'Are they polished?'

'Yes, Mum.'

'Did you wash your feet before putting your shoes on?'

'Yes, Mum.'

A strange question you may think, but I must admit I did not always put my socks and shoes on clean, washed feet. Life at that time was lived by me, indeed by all farm kids around the district, barefooted. The result was that in dry weather and if I was careful not to step in any cow crap while milking, I considered my feet to be clean and washing them unnecessary and merely a waste of time and water. It was different in wet weather, however, when I came back from the cow bails with mud and crap up to my knees. Then the washhouse was used. A small stool (for sitting on) and a tin dish (for the cold water) was kept there to keep the family clean.

'And did you change your shirt?'

'Of course. Fair go, Mum.'

'Which one did you put on?'

'My church shirt. What do you think?'

'It's hard to know with you.'

Don't think that I had an extensive wardrobe of shirts, designer or otherwise, at that time. I had, as most farm kids, the bare minimum – my Sunday shirt, a couple of school shirts and one or two farm shirts. At times I did mix them up and on other occasions I couldn't be bothered changing them when I should have. This kept mum alert.

'And have you combed your hair?'

'Yes, Mum. Surely you can tell. Look at me.'

'OK, but I can't always tell.'

By 8.00am, or shortly after, we were on our way to church, arriving so that there was ample time to socialize, to talk before church proper started. I would turn up with the rest of the family in my dad's old Buick car and join in the usual pre-service activities.

Father would wander up to the shelter shed (yes, the one that is still there) and join the old-timers on the hand-adzed ironbark planks which acted as seats. These were the second-generation members of the district who were now 50 or 60 years old. Here they would find shade from the scorching summer sun, shelter on rainy days and a sunny spot on chilly winter mornings.

They would sit around yarning in groups which would

vary from Sunday to Sunday. There would be Emil, Frank, Gus, Frankie, Otto etc. Originally, they would have been baptized with German names at the beginning of the century (the twentieth) but because of bad feelings towards people of German heritage during World War I and II, these names had been anglicized:

Franz – Frank

Gustav – Gus

Friedrich – Fred

Heinrich – Henry

Wilhelm – Willy or Bill or Billy and so on.

These second-generation settlers would all have been confirmed in the German language. I have framed on my study wall, father's *Erinnerung an den Tag der Confirmation* (my Mum's too), a colourful certificate with all the detail on it written in German. They do not yarn in German as they would have done as kids but now speak only English, some with a distinct German flavour. My wife, Jill, who is from a more British background (75% she will readily boast. This with a touch of German and Spanish) claims that I also speak in a German word order and expression. But I feel that she is not knowing that very good!

Let's join these old farmers.

'Na, Emil, how goes it?'

'Nit so gut, Hermie. Marta's crook and I had to knock old Stumpy one on the head.'

'Gott im Himmel, Emil. He was ya best dog. Vat happened?'

'I tink dat old black snake bit him one on the back leg. He's in the woodheap somewhere and we can't catch da bugger.'

'Didn't see ya in town at the pig sales, Otto?'

'Nah. Had to help Dolf with his corn picking. He thinks there's storms on the way.'

And in this manner the conversations go on, not deeply theological, but keeping up with matters that concern them:

The weather

Price of pigs and corn

The weather

How the sweet spuds are coming on

The weather...

Yes, an hour yarning here and everyone would be up with what was happening in the district.

While the men were sitting in the shed yarning about this and that, some of the women were more migratory in their pre-service manoeuvres. Immediately on arriving at church a number would be seen walking next door to the pastor's residence carrying 'something for the pastor and Mrs Koehler'. This was the generosity of these country folk. These little somethings would be gifts of all manner of fruit and vegetables in season, cakes and biscuits, eggs and plucked chooks and dairy produce.

Deliveries completed, they would join the various groups standing around gossiping. No, no, not gossiping but discussing women's business:

The children

Who's expecting

Upcoming weddings and 21st birthday parties

The children

Cake and biscuit recipes

The children...

And what about the young people (i.e. teenagers, youth,

unmarried males and females)? Yes, there were plenty of these at church too! All the family would be there. They were scattered in segregated groups around the church yard for it was most unusual for male and female to be in the same group. They preferred it this way.

The young fellows could be gathered around a new car on the scene or simply standing in the shade of one of the fig trees talking about what they had been up to, or what they would have liked to have been up to. Possibly girls would be mentioned, definitely farm work or upcoming Luther League events. But nothing religious.

The young girls were also scattered around in groups, with individuals often glancing flirtingly in the direction of one of the young men. Church for them was very much a social event and not to be missed. Here was an opportunity to get dressed up for the morning, for the week probably. Their topics of discussion wouldn't vary much:

Clothes
Boys
Parties
Clothes
Boys
You get the idea!

Us kids? We ran around chasing one another or organizing impromptu games of tiggy, throwing missiles (small stones, sticks, clods of dirt, fallen figs off the trees) at one another or any of the older boys who ventured near. There were also trees to climb but only those out of sight of the parents. Generally, we were hellbent on getting dirty, which was not popular with our parents for we all would be in our Sunday best. With shoes on too, which made tree climbing much harder. We were releasing energy so that we might sit quietly and still in church for the next one and a half to two hours – a big ask but something that parents would have appreciated.

Then it was into church. There was no bell here to be rung but the people generally knew when it was time to go inside. They could have heard Sarah (or whoever) playing the old pedal organ. When these musical notes from Sarah echoed out through the weather-board timber walls everyone would slowly move towards one of the three doors which lead into the church. Most would sit in the same pew from one week to the next. In this way it was easy to see who was missing.

The elders would sit in the front middle pew. They would walk in and take their place leaving the rest of their families to sit separately; and their wives to look after the kids during the service. Some would doze off during the sermon, something they could never have done if surrounded by their children. One individual was noted for his snoring from time to time. The congregation members and the Pastor were accepting of this. He worked hard on his farm and as he would remind everyone; Sunday was a day of rest. All would be awake to attend the first table of communion.

Talking about communion; that's when the church service really went for a long time. Just think about it.

No one was allowed to help the Pastor.

There was no continuous communion, and there were hundreds to get through. He had to give the bread and then give the wine to each individual at the communion rail. Then he would give the blessing to each table of about twelve

8. Church at Ten O'clock

before the next one filed up. People knew which table they would be on because they had to announce their intention before the start of service. Probably so that no non-Lutherans slipped in! (The Lutheran Church at that time practised closed communion). Communion services were long affairs and I'm sure that most of us kids were happy that it only came around once a month.

Back to us kids in church. It was tough sitting through the whole service, which was really directed towards the adults. One needed some distractions.

'Psst. Mum! Have to go for a p.'

'I told you to go before we left home.'

'I did, didn't I?'

'Well, you shouldn't have to go again so soon.'

'Really got to go again, Mum. It's coming out. I can't hold it.'

'Off you go then, but make sure you come straight back.'

'Yes, Mum.'

Having received reluctant permission I would go out, wander slowly up to the toilet and stand behind it for a while. Then I would toss a few stones at the Mickeys (birds) and walk around the hall. That excursion completed I would then walk solemnly back to my pew with a feigned look of relief on my face. Mum would welcome me with a stony frown. This strategy worked only once during a service, and not every week either. Mums can remember.

What to do next? Let your eyes wander around the church and catch the eye of a friend – or wishfully the eyes of an imagined girlfriend – and screw up your nose. But that was soon noticed and stopped, generally with a slight tug on the ear to get the eyes to the front. Sure, this could be tried a few times, but the tugs would become less slight as the service progressed.

Then it was up to just gazing. Finding joins in the VJ pine boards which lined the inside of the church was a time-consuming activity. They were long, unpainted boards. Still are. Later in life I became quite envious of those boards for I developed a love of timber and there was beauty in that hoop pine. There is in this old timber church generally. It had been noticed by many others who, after they had visited, would most likely say, 'What a lovely old church!'

I couldn't gaze forever for my neck would become sore from looking up, but the service would eventually come to an end. The worshippers would file out one of the three – now exit – doors. Most would head straight to their cars and drive off home. There was very little standing around, discussing the sermon or simply talking like before the service. No cups of tea and biscuits either. Soon the large weatherboard church was left alone with its pine trees, fig trees and eucalypts, its cows and cornfields.

Everyone was anxious to get home for dinner.

9.

Old Blacky

BLACKY WAS MY HORSE. In saying this, I have to acknowledge that before then at various times throughout his life he was also Terry's horse, Ron's horse and Merle's horse. He was what you might say a hand-me-down horse. As I was the youngest member of our family, he eventually ended up with me. All the children in my family – and we were four – had learnt to ride on Blacky. It was a simple process and worked like this: The neophyte would begin his rider training on Blacky and when his apprenticeship was completed, and his riding proficiency allowed progress to a higher level of horse, Blacky was passed down to the next in line chronologically.

I don't know how he felt about this lot in life, but outwardly he took it in his stride and readily accepted the next youngster waiting to learn to ride. Perhaps not so readily. Acceptance followed only after testing the mettle of this new owner with a few unexpected bites on the backside while he (or she, in the case of my sister) was bending over tightening the girth strap or an unexpected sidestep or pigroot while slowly ambling along.

As the youngest sibling, I probably had ownership for the longest, for I did not move on to a more advanced level of steed. No, it was not a lack of competence, but rather an economic consideration on the part of my father. Why have Blacky standing around doing nothing – nothing but eating, that is – with no further family member waiting to be taught to ride? Also, I would be leaving for boarding school and would not need my own better quality horse (Horses were not allowed at my boarding school and I had to be content with a bicycle). So Blacky and I were stuck with each other. It was during this time that we started calling him Old Blacky rather than Blacky.

While being Old Blacky he became cantankerous at times and was often abused (verbally) by most members of my family, using their own individual expressions. In spite of this occasional abuse, he was a fine horse – and yes, even a fine **old** horse – and throughout his working life he remained faithful and true to the novices on his back who were learning the fine art of horsemanship. Well, let me rephrase that. They were just learning to ride! And like all of us he also had his shortcomings.

Blacky could hardly be regarded as a tall, upstanding animal. My brother had graduated to be the owner of a proud, chestnut gelding. Its rippling muscles shouted strength. It stood at sixteen hands. Blacky could more accurately be described as chubby, flabby in parts and would need extra thick horseshoes to be honestly listed at thirteen hands. Even so he could be an aggressive little beggar whose bite was certainly worse than his neigh, especially when near hay. He would always end up with more than his share. This added to his rotundity and the fact that everyone considered him a lazy horse did not help his temperament. My brother's 'You lazy, little bugger' never failed to bring an abrupt turning of the head and a diabolic glint in his eyes.

But let's be honest. It was not that he was lazy but rather he had grown used to his slower pace of life because he was not needed very often. One would seldom see him racing around the paddocks as the other horses loved doing. His most strenuous exercise was slowly trotting away from me when I was trying to catch him to saddle him up to go riding somewhere. Oh, and racing up to the feed trough when fodder was being handed out.

He was cunning enough to realise what was in store for him when he saw me approaching with a bridle in my hand. He would immediately turn around and trot away. I would normally have to enlist my brother to help corner him. That was often a much more difficult task than it sounds, for he usually claimed to have more important jobs to do than to help catch 'that lazy little bugger'.

I did have a plan B which I used, but I used it so often that it became my plan A. If I were to approach him with a handful of lucerne hay he would come to meet me with his mouth already grinding from side to side. Clearly his gluttony was a stronger driving force than his laziness.

This then became my strategy for catching him. While he was eating my bribe, I would grab hold of his mane and swing up on his back. This is where his height of thirteen hands came in handy – for me. Once on his back I was in control. You see, he had been trained to accept an obsequious position when someone was on his back. Once there, with the right number of kicks with my heels and pulling handfuls of his mane, which I might add was thinning out at this stage of his life, I could cajole him over to the paddock gate which was waiting with the bridle.

The effort which was required to catch the beast probably was the main reason I rode my bike to school on most days. This was more readily available, usually lying on the back lawn where I had left it the day before when I arrived home from school. I was continually being reminded that this was not where the bike should be. I knew that and didn't have to be reminded all the time. I remember that I would always come up with some excuse for failing to put it under the house where it belonged.

On the other hand, I really did enjoy riding Old Blacky to school. It was an effortless experience (more so for me than him) especially if my dad or one of my brothers had been kind enough to catch him and saddle him up. Were he ready to be ridden, I would swing up into the saddle, my schoolbag on my back, let a few clicks out of the side of my mouth, kick him lightly in the flanks with my feet in the stirrups, and off we would go. School buses? Who needed them! I had my own private taxi.

The 'going off' would not be a speedy going off, but quite the opposite. By the time he had been passed on to me through all those hands who had to catch and saddle him, he had become somewhat of a reluctant starter. But once realising the inevitability of the day ahead he would slowly amble his way to school without guidance or any more encouragement from me. All I had to do was to sit and go through my times tables. Actually, that's not quite true. I don't believe I ever

9. Old Blacky

learnt my times tables riding Blacky to school.

From time to time, I would have gone through some of the poems we had to learn by heart. Our teacher, Mr Barton, was a stickler for learning poems, usually those found in our School Reader. Once learnt, never forgotten.

I love a sunburnt country,
A land of sweeping plains,
Of ragged mountain ranges,
Of drought and flooding rains.

And then there was Sir Walter Scott's, Young Lochinvar:

O! young Lochinvar is come out of the west;
Through all the wide Border, his steed was the best;

This poem, with its anapestic beat was better suited for the homeward journey when I could more easily spur Blacky into a gallop. Yes, he could gallop, which gave rhythm to my poetry recital, but never did I imagine myself as that daring knight, Lochinvar, carrying off his fair maiden, Ellen, on the back of his charger (Blacky's back? Hardly!).

Mostly, I would just sit there in a daze and look around at whatever there was to be seen.

That could be Uncle Otto from next door shifting his irrigation pipes. I would give him a cheery wave and shout 'Good Morning, Uncle Otto!'. He would look up but not wave back for he had both hands around the pipe he was shifting. And he couldn't return my greeting for he always had a pipe in his mouth.

Maybe a couple of Bill Tillach's heifer calves were out on the road. He was well-known for his fences. I would spend a few minutes trying to turn them around and set them off in the right direction, back to where they belonged. I saw this as doing the right thing for my neighbour.

Then there were ample numbers of birds to look at. And I was a keen bird watcher. The starlings would fill up whole rows of electric light wires. Or if not them, there would be rows of finches sitting up there – red beaks, zebras and double bars. Quails would be darting about in the grass in the water table. Peewees and magpies were there looking for their mid-morning snack while their black-and-white ibis friends would be picking their way through the moister areas. The ubiquitous sparrows could not be missed.

I remember how once this bountiful bird life gave me the idea of taking my shanghai with me on the horse to school. I noticed how Old Blacky slowly mooching along would not disturb the birds from what they were doing. After all he was just an animal like they, and I as a rider, would seem to be part of him. I figured that I would be taken quite close to my prey and should easily be able to bag a few.

I had lined up a sparrow sitting on a fence post just ahead, pulled back the rubbers and let fly. The slingshot stone missed the target – not by much I must add – but the shanghai's pouch flicked Blacky's ear. This startled him up out of his peaceful morning walk. He gave a completely unexpected root, and I ended up on my backside, or whatever, in the grass in the water-table, with quails scuttling off for their lives and the sparrow flying off unharmed. Startled as he was, Blacky also ran off, but not for long. After a short distance he stopped,

9. Old Blacky

turned around and looked at me probably wondering why I had done something so stupid. I was able to walk up to him, grab the reins, swing back up on the saddle and then continue my way to school.

I had planned not to tell my parents about this slight mishap in being bucked off my horse. Most horse riders find it hard to admit to such a thing. But that was not to be! Mum was first to notice that something was amiss.

'What on earth have you been doing with your schoolbag?' she asked when first laying eyes on it when I arrived home that afternoon. I must point out that it was a fairly flimsy bag made out of some sort of hard cardboard material.

'Why? What do you mean?' I asked innocently.

'It's all out of shape, as if you've been rolling around on it,' she explained.

I had noticed that it was a bit skewwhiff when I arrived at school, but I had thought that I had pushed it back into its rectangular shape for no one to notice. But Mum had an eye for the out-of-shape.

'I must have rolled on it when I fell off the horse going to school.' I hoped that this explanation would suffice.

'What? You fell off Blacky? How could that happen?' Our whole family knew that under normal circumstances one just did not fall off Blacky.

'Well, he got a fright, gave a buck I wasn't expecting and I went flying.'

Mum was persistent in her interrogation. 'What frightened him? Getting an answer out of you is like drawing teeth. Why don't you tell me the whole story?'

And so with my co-operation, and after a few more probing

questions (and I was loath to tell a lie) she was soon aware of the whole sorry story. 'I'm sure your father won't be happy when he hears about this. Trying to shoot birds on your way to school! I mean to say!'

Yes, an ominous conclusion to our discussions.

Being a basically honest child I had to own up to my dad that Old Blacky had bucked me off and why. As I suspected and as Mum had rightly anticipated, he was not impressed that I was taking my shanghai to school and trying to shoot birds on the way. This did not surprise me. He gave me a good whack around the backside. This did not surprise me either.

There were two different roads by which I could go to school. From our house I would go down our side road to the corner, about a quarter of a mile away. Here I could either go straight ahead or turn to the left. Both of these options would eventually arrive at my primary school. I could also turn right at the corner, but this would take me to the local town of Gatton and not to the school. It would also get me to **Lower** Tent Hill State School but as I mentioned earlier, I did not go there because we lived on the wrong side of the road.

I would always leave Blacky make up his own mind as to which way he would go to school. He knew where we were going. Some days he would go straight ahead and others he would turn left and take that route. His choices were, to me at least, completely random. Maybe he had reasons for making the selections which he did, but he kept them to himself. He would never turn right to go into Gatton. I don't believe he was ever in Gatton, so he probably didn't know that it even existed.

Maybe he was aware of where the best roadside snacks were to be found. He did consider it not inappropriate to

9. Old Blacky

stop every now and then to have a few mouthfuls of juicy grass which grew alongside the bitumen road. I saw this as preparing for the eight hours of fasting that lay ahead. He would have known that there was not much to be had in the horse paddock at school. Fasting was not popular with Blacky! The horse paddock was a small area of the creek bank which adjoined the school yard. It was always grazed thoroughly bare by the pupils' horses. Here I would take off his saddle and bridle which would then be placed in a shed which had been especially erected for that purpose. He would then be free to spend the rest of the school day in the company of like-minded scholarly horses.

When the school day was completed I would have to resaddle my means of transport which would then find its own way home with me sitting quietly in the saddle revising the lessons of the day. No, not really. Saying some poetry and dreaming of having a charger like Young Lochinvar? Perhaps. The trip home was always a little quicker than the journey to school. Blacky knew that he would be entitled to a generous portion of lucerne hay for his day's duties.

The mounted shanghai episode was not the only time Blacky thought fit to buck me off. This other time I consider he did it without provocation. I had ridden down to the irrigation paddock to fetch the cows. It was my dad's animal husbandry practice to have the milking cows graze for an hour every day on the lucerne crop. This highly nutritious food would boost their milk and cream output. The herd's hour of grazing was up and I was to go down and fetch them. I went down on horse-back – Blacky's back. Our cattle dog, Bluey, soon had them out of the lucerne paddock and onto the road.

Rather than chase the cows from behind, I rode in front of them. They had been trained to follow and they preferred this to being chased from behind. With a few bovine-sounding 'come-on, come-ons', they were happily following Blacky and me and Bluey home. Every little while I would turn round to make sure my charges were playing the game and following.

I had an idea: Rather than twisting around all the time and possibly wrenching my neck, why didn't I sit on the horse backwards? I was riding with a saddle, but this should pose no problem if I sat behind it. Blacky knew the way home so he needed no bridle and bit to guide him. Good idea, I decided. I kneeled up on the saddle, turned around and sat down on his bare back rather close to his tail. I had no sooner sat down than he bucked – 'pigrooted' is probably the technical term – and I went flying. I had unintentionally touched him in a ticklish spot and he reacted accordingly. I ended up on my backside in the paspalum grass in the water-table.

9. Old Blacky

Bluey came and licked my face which was his normal reaction when I was down at his level. Blacky merely stopped and looked back at me with a sympathetic look on his face which seemed to be saying, 'That was a silly thing to do.' The cows all kept walking past, not at all interested in my fall. I got back on my horse, facing to the front, and continued taking the cows back to their home grazing paddock. That night, at the tea table, when I told my family about it, they all laughed and my dad said, 'That was a silly thing to do.'

Even with all his shortcomings, and his height was not really one of these, Blacky was a loved member of the equine family on our farm. Sure, the big, strong Clydesdales would probably talk about him behind his back and push him out of the way if they didn't really want him to get those few extra mouthfuls of hay, but generally he was left in peace. He was the elder statesman of the group and this would have counted for something despite his stature.

His back had taught all four of us children in the family to ride. I was the youngest and so the last to need his tutorage. Time was catching up with him. His age was becoming obvious, especially in his mane and on his rump. Soon 'Blacky' would be an inappropriate name, for his previously black, glossy hairs would be outnumbered by the grey ones. But one could never call him Greyey, Hoary or any other silly, unimaginative name!

Nestled somewhere within his cavernous tummy beat a large heart which did not seem to deteriorate with age. It was a heart that would not shy away from a challenge.

My neighbour, Clem, had a young, spritely pony which he also would ride to school from time to time. On these occasions we would ride along together. Clem's horse was never content with the slow amblings of Blacky and was always anxious to move the pace along. His promptings would usually fall on deaf, unresponsive ears.

Although racing the two horses was strictly forbidden by both sets of parents, we figured that the occasional short contest would fall outside the concept of racing and would not really count as disobedience.

'So is he up to it today?' Clem might ask.

'This old fellow is always ready and willing,' would be my boastful reply, speaking for Blacky.

'To Steinhardt's gate then. Go when you are ready.'

With a quiet word in Blacky's ear to wake him from his daydreaming, and then a shout of 'Go! Go! Go!' accompanied by a few sharp kicks to his flanks, he was off, wondering why the rush.

Very soon Clem's horse, Pearl, was abreast and then a few strides ahead. It was at this point that Blacky realised a race was on and his determination was soon apparent to me in the saddle.

Every muscle was straining as he sought to keep up with his flighty neighbour. But alas, the resolve was there but the short legs, having grown a little wearier with age, were unable to do the job. An enjoyable short, relatively swift ride for me, but for Blacky another race lost.

'Blacky,' I would console him, 'you were not born to be a racehorse. You were meant to be our tutor, teaching us how to ride.'

Then I went off to boarding school and my days of horse riding basically came to an end. I don't remember whether it was when I came home for the first or second term holidays that my father said that they had gotten rid of Blacky.

No! I didn't break down into uncontrollable sobbing.

'Oh? Where to? You didn't have him put down, did you?' I asked, alarm showing in my voice.

My father replied. 'No, don't worry! Kevin Hoger from church was looking around for a small horse. His young fellow is ready to start learning to ride. I gave Blacky to them.'

So Blacky continued his life's calling as a hand-me-down horse. To Kevin's young lad, Melvyn, however, he would not be regarded as a hand-me-down. He would be his first, brand-new horse, his pride and joy.

As my horse, there was never any great attachment between us. Sure I, or rather we, looked after him, gave him the odd brushing down and saw to it that he had a comfortable existence while he was with us. He was, however, just a horse which had a role to play on the farm.

That role was completed when I went off to school and so it made sense that he go where he could be useful. During holidays I still had to fetch the cows in for milking morning and evening. I now had to go on foot and not ride the horse (I would actually run). This was child's play compared to the training runs my sport's captain at school made his team members do!

I had begun a new phase in my life. So had Blacky.

10.

A Child's Christmas

Part A – Preparation

FLYING FOXES, AN UPSIDE-DOWN Y and shouting (understand that as singing) out loudly, but in time and perfect pitch, 'Shepherds quake at the sight', are just some of the things that pop into my mind when recalling Christmas as a child. A strange collection of memories, you may be thinking. Shouting out a Christmas carol is the only one that makes any sense. Perhaps you would think that, and if I were to include crepe paper, China flat peaches and a glass of sarsaparilla, then the list, rather than becoming more enlightening, would probably become even more unusual and baffling for you.

What about Santa Claus, Christmas trees and stockings, plum pudding laden with mixed fruit, threepences and rum, not to mention family fights? Don't these enter the equation? Well, yes and no; but mainly no. Initially, absolutely no. I would have to be reminded of these references, the others not. As for family fights? No, not at Christmas time. To tell you the truth, not at all.

10. A Child's Christmas

'You've got to be kidding!'

'No, not really.'

'You were indeed a lucky child,' you might reply.

I would have to agree. I had no worries about what Santa might bring me, something which seems to occupy many children's minds in the weeks, or months, leading up to Christmas these days. We had no Christmas stockings to hang up on the fireplace under the chimney. We had no fireplace and the chimney leading up from the wood stove in the kitchen was too small for Santa to slide down. Hang a stocking there and it would catch alight next time Mum lit the stove.

And a pile of colourfully-wrapped, hopeful presents under a Christmas tree? No, we had no Christmas tree at home. There was a high, decorated tree in our church and that sufficed. It had real candles on it which were lit for the Christmas eve children's service; there were sparklers too. But I am getting ahead of myself.

Strange as it may appear to the twenty-first century child, the focus of my childhood Christmases was not holidays I might go on or presents which I was hoping to receive. It was the Sunday School program presented (performed, would perhaps be a better way of expressing it) in our packed church on the night before Christmas. Christmas day and many of those other regular things which people associate with this time, fade into insignificance compared with that once-a-year Christmas eve event. To me, as a child, that was Christmas.

The evening of December the 24th was (still is) an immovable date on the church year calendar. Easter moves around from one year to the next. Ascension Day, when is that? And the 18th Sunday after Pentecost is hardly a day to stick in one's mind. Christmas eve is on another level altogether. Everyone knew from one year to the next exactly when it would be. On this night the children of the congregation would once again, in action, word and song, present the good tidings of great joy to their parents and friends and all the other locals who would roll up at the church to... But I am getting ahead of myself again. It seems that I just can't wait for Christmas eve!

Already, weeks before the magic evening – I don't remember exactly how many: five, six, maybe? – the many-paged Children's Christmas Service Program would appear. This was prepared, I now know, by someone high up in the church hierarchy. Back then, who wrote it or where it came from, was not a child's concern. It had arrived. It was here! Some years even in technicolour. Well, printed on green or yellow foolscap paper. With members of the various Sunday School classes standing almost to attention, it was reverently handed out

10. A Child's Christmas

by Sarah, Joan, Percy, Alan, Dorothy and the others Sunday School teachers.

So many? Yes, indeed. We were not a small group which would barely fill one pew in the church. No! We were many. A multitude one might say.

When I was a child, my local congregation had a membership of over 400 souls and these were not only the elderly. The elderly were in the minority, for many at that time did not live long enough to join the ranks of the elderly. The congregation was the aggregate of all the whole families from the grandparents (small in number) through middle age (well up in numbers), teenagers (high in numbers), to kids and babies (running around everywhere – not the babies). The church was a multi-generational affair.

After the program had been handed out the efforts of the Sunday School teachers and children for the next five, or six, or however many weeks, revolved around the content of this program – the teachers to teach it and the kids to learn it. The polished article would then be presented errorless (remembering that mistakes can occur) to the congregation and visitors who turned up for the evening. No reading off sheets of green or yellow (I can also remember blue one year), and no being prompted by teachers. No. Everything – songs, Bible references, individual items, the whole story – had to be known off pat.

Then to ensure that this would be the case, for three weeks leading up to Christmas eve, the Sunday School became the Saturday School. Yes, on Saturday morning all the children would turn up at the church hall to practise their own little sections and get the whole presentation into shape. There was more time available on a Saturday morning. So instead of going to the local state school, as during the week, the kids would head off in a different direction. This was during the Christmas school holidays and one morning at school – Saturday School – wasn't seen as a bad thing.

They would ride their bikes, their horses or simply walk to the church hall. Being driven in the family car? No way! If you can walk to the local school (and most did) you can walk to Saturday School.

I rode my horse Blacky. I started off my journey not by going down the road as if heading off to normal school but up the hill past Uncle Otto Krenske's place. Here Clem, around my age, just a few months older, would join me on his horse. It was a surveyed road which had never been built and so consisted of a rutted track, usually overgrown with grass, scrub and bushes on both sides. Therein lay the attraction for both Blacky and myself. Clem, too, of course. It was here, nestled secretly in this lateral mini jungle, that the wild plums grew. These small bushes which would often develop into vines climbing up the small trees would bear edible (for us young boys) fruit, rosy red or plump purple, sweet and juicy with just a hint of tart. We knew the location of the best plants and so our ride was being continually interrupted as we stopped to sample a few more wild plums. Blacky would also appreciate these stops. He had time to grab a mouthful or two of the green grass of his choice.

The wild plums were yummy but the main highlights growing among the bushes along the side of the unmade road were two China flat peach trees. The fruit would ripen in the weeks leading up to Christmas and even today I cannot think of the Holy Season without thinking about China flat peaches. Oh, that soft, juicy, white flesh! Oh, that special, unique feeling of sweet juice running down my chin. We also had a couple of trees at home – one in the orchard and the other down on the cultivation beside the well. Stewed peached and dumplings was a favourite pudding in the weeks before Christmas.

Blacky must have known exactly where the two trees on the way to Saturday School were located for invariably he would stop adjacent to them and start munching grass. Or maybe it was the particularly succulent grass at these two places which caused him to stop. We knew where the trees were located and were lucky that the fruit fly did not. We were able to eat the fruit without worrying about the fruit fly maggots which might be lurking within.

Pick a soft, ripe specimen, break it in two, flick out the seed and one has two unforgettable pieces of peach to eat and enjoy. And another. And another. Young boys just do not know when to stop.

But we had to stop and move on. Up the hill further, past Albert Krenske's place. No need to stop here for his kids were too old to go to Sunday School. Then down the hill and up the next one. Plenty of wild plums growing here too, but enough is enough.

We would then arrive at a surveyed T-junction. We could either take the track to the left or the one to the right. We would take neither but go straight ahead passing through Bill Krenske's property. You have probably noticed that there are plenty of Krenskes around here. Mind you, had we taken the track to the left at the T-junction we would have come to Gus Krenske's farm.

To get into Bill Krenske's place we had to first dismount, one of us that is, and open the gap in the fence to get into his corn paddock. This was not an easy task because his gaps were always tightly strained and it was difficult for young lads like us to undo the loop holding the barbed-wire gap in place. And then it had to be closed once we passed through. If left open and Bill found out (and uncannily he usually did) one could expect a good kick up the backside. However, as country boys we knew that gaps and gates should not be left open. There were animals of one sort or another on all the farms and most were very good at finding gates and gaps which had been left open.

We would go around the growing corn but Blacky would always try to edge a little closer to the cornstalks and take the opportunity of grabbing a mouthful. The ultimate opportunist where food was concerned was my Blacky. He was a chubby little fellow and this was why.

Once through (or should I say, around) the corn field we would go into the house block. Yes, through a gap which was always tightly closed. Once through, the first stop was at the house dam to give the horses a drink. They would have to stand in the hot sun for the next few hours and this drink was a must.

Our next stop was calling into the Krenske house (Bill Krenske, that is) to pick up Selly and his little sister. They would usually wait so that they could walk beside us for the rest of the way to the church, probably half a mile at that time.

But first we had to go inside to say hello to Aunty Tilly, Bill's wife and Clem's aunt; not mine, she was my great-aunt. Saturday morning was generally baking day throughout the district. Clem and I had an ulterior motive for wanting to say hello to Aunty Tilly. Her first batch of biscuits would be well out of the oven by the time we arrived and would have had time to cool off enough to be eaten. We would be disappointed not to score a few to go with the wild plums and China flat peaches which had sustained us during the morning so far.

Finally, we arrived at the church hall and tied up our horses to the side fence. Who said going to Saturday School was boring?

We would take the saddles off and place them in the shade of a tree. There was no horse paddock at the church like at my school, and so Blacky and Clem's horse, and others which had arrived from other directions, would have to wait in the sun until it was time to head home. But they could stand proud, knowing that they had played their part in the events leading up to our Christmas.

For us kids the yuletide adventure would continue. The Saturdays would roll round, varying little from one week to the next but all arriving at the church hall which would always be full of the joyous sounds of children chanting, singing, and talking when they weren't supposed to. As any actor will tell you, the practicing and the rehearsing are necessary preliminaries to delivering an errorless presentation. All this was part of the preparation which helped hasten the coming of Christmas.

Soon Christmas eve would be upon us. Oh, the excitement of it all!

11.

A Child's Christmas

Part B - Presentation

THE CHILDREN'S CHRISTMAS PROGRAM to be presented in front of the whole congregation, plus many other visitors, had been well-drilled and finely tuned. Lines had been learnt to perfection, individual and group segments polished to shining and carols practised until they flowed without fault. Angelic, you might say. Now for the big night. What possibly could go wrong? Yes, this for most of us was what Christmas was all about. Absent was the commercialisation which one sees today, and which makes Christmas a humbug for so many. For us, Christmas boiled down to presenting the story of the birth of Jesus as told in the Bible – an animated nativity scene.

The sun was barely setting as the young participants began arriving at the church with their parents and friends. All were decked out in their sartorial splendour; girls in their pretty frocks and the boys in white shirts (some would be less white by the time the service began), and where possible clean pants

11. A Child's Christmas

and shoes (Yes, I know it's not Sunday, but you must wear your shoes. You are going to church).

This time also saw the arrival of flying foxes, also known as fruit bats, who in their thousands were flying over the church on the way to their feeding grounds. One could stand and gaze with head looking up until one's neck got sore watching the black bats glide past. Most did. Some didn't, for here in the church grounds these had reached their goal for the evening. Surrounding the church were several Moreton Bay fig trees, huge affairs, loaded with small fig-like fruit. And the flying foxes loved them. Thinking back, a probable reason for our China flat peaches not being attacked by these fruit bats was that they were in such a hurry to get to the church figs.

Having landed in the fig trees, the bats were noisily (very noisily indeed, for they are squabbling creatures) enjoying their dinner. Or could this be regarded as their breakfast? They had spent the whole day hanging around in the colony sleeping and this was the first meal of their day.

To fill in time before the start of the evening's proceedings, many of the boys would congregate under the fig trees trying to scare the bats away by making more noise than they did. This was a fruitless task. The bats seemed unmoved by the noise coming up from below, did not fly away but would merely chase their companions from a nearby bunch of figs and claim it for themselves. This they would probably do even without interference from a group of boys below. Our church bats seemed to be very selfish and quarrelsome, hardly in keeping with the Christian message. And at Christmas time, too!

In their greediness or as a message of disdain they would let drop pieces of uneaten fruit and other waste material which they had expelled from their own selves. Inevitably, some of these droppings would land on the boys' white shirts.

'Mum, there's shit on my shirt.'

Mums were unamused.

'You should know better than to stand under the fig trees with all those flying foxes in them!'

As I indicated previously; Flying foxes form an important part of my memories of childhood Christmas. They have left their mark.

Eventually, at 7 o'clock, we were all rounded up and escorted inside; marched in, would be more accurate. This was to ensure that each participant ended up sitting in the correct position, most necessary for the smooth running of the program, for its continuity. The normal seating in the whole south-west portion of the church was reorganized, the raised section in front of the altar filled with pews to seat this show with a cast of thousands, or so it seemed.

Once the children were seated the evening's program could begin. First of all, the candles on the Christmas tree – real wax candles – had to be lit. This was the job of one of the elders of the congregation, usually Emil. Why Emil? Who would know, for they all smoked a pipe, and all would have had a packet of matches in their pocket.

Emil would approach the tree with a box of wax matches in his hand, and all eyes in the church, especially those of the children, were focused on him. The lighting would never run smoothly because small, new candles were always used and these were difficult to light. Not only did Emil have to concentrate on the wick at the top of the candle but he also had to be aware that a false move could set the whole tree alight.

11. A Child's Christmas

After many matches, a burnt finger or two and the same number of mutters (very unchristian ones I would imagine) most of the candles would be burning brightly.

'What about that one above your head, Uncle Emil?'

'Shh! You're in church.'

'And there's another one you missed. Behind the blue angel.'

The church was never burnt down. One year the tree did catch fire, something noticed by everyone in the church, but the fire was immediately extinguished.

The sparklers were only lit at the end of the service. That remains my image of a real Christmas tree – an actual cone-shaped pine tree, with a star on top, candles lighting up the bottom section (no candles on the upper portion for Emil could not reach so high) and sparklers creating the spectacular finale.

After a few brief opening words from the pastor (he would keep his main message for the next day) it was over to us kids singing carols, quoting Bible texts, relating the Christmas story and generally entertaining the congregation with our enthusiasm.

To provide some visual appeal during the children's presentation there were a number of segments where a line of children would, in turn, starting from the audience's left, recite a poem or Biblical fact while holding up a letter of the alphabet. At the end of the segment there would be a key word spelt out such as: C H R I S T or M A N G E R. Those bearing letters had to be seated in the correct position. Bad spelling was not acceptable.

I remember one particular Christmas eve very clearly. I was still in a lower class and a small group of us was to spell out a message to the congregation:

'J is for **J**esus whom we welcome today', Kevin bravely shouted out for all the congregation to hear.

'O is for the **o**ne who came as a baby,' Peter's voice was equally as loud.

Next was my turn and, on queue, I held up my designated letter eager to shout out my message. But everyone started laughing. I felt embarrassed. What were they laughing at? I had my letter held up high for all to see. Peter, beside me, looked and then poked me in the ribs. 'Your Y is upside down.'

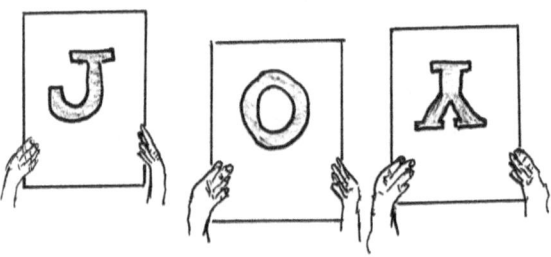

A quick flick of my wrist and then,

'Y He came for **y**ou and me and everyone.'

Then followed a lusty rendition of *Joy to the world, the Lord is come* ...

The whole program was interspersed with a number of the best-known Christmas carols: *While Shepherds watched their flocks by night*; *Come hither, ye children*; *O thou holiest*; the list goes on. Don't forget that we had to know them all by heart!

And not forgetting *Silent night, holy night*.

Yes, *Silent night, holy night*. Many memories here. Sarah, the teacher in charge of the music, had a special way for us to sing this old favourite. The first verse was to be sung very quietly, sort of setting the mood, creating an atmosphere. In the second verse, the first line, *Silent night, holy night*, was again pp; but the second line, *Shepherds quake at the sight*, was to be given loud and clear, with an emphasis on the loud. We loved doing this double volume; fff indeed (fortississimo). And the church shook.

Babies woke up and started screaming and crying. The dozing elders jumped, awakened from their slumber. 'Is the last day upon us?'

This would happen every year, for there could be no Christmas without *Silent night, holy night*. The people would always forget what was coming.

After the age-old Christmas story had once again been told, after the Pastor had pronounced a Christmas blessing on all those present, it was time for the children to crowd around their individual teachers who had emerged from somewhere within the congregation each bearing a box overflowing with. . .

But wait. Let's go back a few months before Christmas.

At this time, October probably, a rightly appointed man for the task had been going around all families at church collecting for the Children's Christmas Fund. All knew that they would be approached and were happy enough to part with a few hard-earned pounds, some with only ten bob or so, this being Christmas after all, and seeing it was for the kids. Part of this money would go towards buying suitable books and all the children would receive one, complete with a sticker inside the front cover, with their name and congratulating them on a great year.

I recently came across one such book on my shelves, not mine, but from well before my time. How it got there I have no idea. It had an 'Awarded to' sticker and on it was written:

'Freda Hoger. For obtaining highest marks in the Ropeley Lutheran Sunday School, 1924', and then signed by the pastor of the day, H.E.Temme. The book was a hard cover copy of *The Pilgrim's Progress* by John Bunyan. I wonder did Freda ever get round to reading it? Who knows? Can't ask Aunty Freda (yes, she really was my aunt) for she died some time ago.

I wonder how many people today have ever heard of *The Pilgrim's Progress* let alone read it?

Back to the Christmas fund. After the books were paid for, the balance of the money went towards buying lollies for all the children of the congregation.

My father was often the person nominated to buy the lollies. What a job! He and a few others (connoisseurs of the sweet tooth) would drive up to Toowoomba, call in at the local sweets manufacturer and bring home boxes and boxes of lollies. For some reason I always associate the name Mervyn Dynes, or some similar name, with lollies in Toowoomba. I have no idea why. Perhaps he was the actual manufacturer.

Father's old Buick would arrive back from Toowoomba loaded with a great variety of sweets: hard jubes, soft jubes, caramel twists, liquorice all-sorts, milk bottles, hard-boiled bull's eyes. Oh please stop! I'm salivating. Then there were also conversation lollies.

Yes, conversation lollies. These were small slabs of various shapes with short messages written on them. Once having received the packet full of sweets many would root around to find these. If lucky, there would be one suitable to pass to a possible girlfriend before the evening was over: 'Your smile is sweet', 'Sometime soon?', 'Always thinking of you', 'Remember me?' Oh, the literary giants who came up with these conversations.

11. A Child's Christmas

As a child who seldom had lollies to eat, it was very difficult for me living in a house with the lounge room stacked full of boxes of them. But they were all tightly closed with tamperproof string – or so I was given to believe – and I was basically an honest, trustworthy boy. I waited, and waited, and waited, knowing that eventually at Christmas eve I would receive my packet.

There in the lounge room they would remain until lolly-bagging day when they would be packed into the many bags destined to sweeten Christmas eve for all the children in the district.

Since weeks before, various women of the congregation, had been busily turning brown paper bags into colourful containers. With a range of colourful crepe paper, paste and ribbons, the plain paper bags became cheerful messengers inviting the children to draw the strings open wide and enjoy. These bags came in various sizes – large, medium, small and baby – designed for the various age groups. No conversation lollies for the baby's packets.

The boxes which the teachers were now taking up to their excited groups were overflowing with books and colourful bags of sweets. 'Now don't forget that you are not to open your bag until you are out of the church!'

'Yes, Alan.'

And Alan, together with the other teachers, started handing out a reward for the year of Sunday/Saturday School attendance. No tests in my day to see who would come first in the class as in Aunty Freda's time. We were all winners. And the Christmas eve service ended with each child lovingly clutching an unopened book and a half-eaten bag of lollies.

For me and my family it was then into the old Buick and home, where the celebration would continue. For Christmas, Father would always collect a dozen (twelve) large bottles (one pint, not like today's large bottles) of soft drink from the local Soft Drink and Cordial Works in Gatton. Was it Bishops? I forget. Christmas was one of the few times throughout the year when we had soft drink in the house. This was the era before Coke.

The custom was that when we arrived home from church on Christmas eve, we would be allowed a glass of soft drink. I would have a glass of sarsaparilla. The joy of Christmas was complete.

12.

Hop... Two, Three

PHYS ED?

Oh! Physical Education: stuff like running, hopping, jumping, lifting and throwing?

You've gotta be kidding. We didn't go to school to do those sorts of things. We were doing things like that all the time at home. School was for the three rs.

Looking back, I don't think Phys Ed really rated a mention in the curriculum of my primary school. If it did, Mr Barton kept it a secret. He would have seen exercise, of the physical kind, as the last thing we country kids needed to do at school. Why take time away from doing sums, learning poetry or parsing sentences to do something which we were all doing out of school time anyway?

Exercise of the book kind. That was a different matter, because we all had to have our exercise books and make sure we used them. No, one couldn't write enough compositions: *Working for Mum; My best friend; My favourite colour; My last holiday*. The list of titles is endless and so imaginative. That

my school

is what school was all about, trying to make a composition on *My Favourite Colour* gripping and exciting, neatly written without any spelling errors. I couldn't do that today, after eight decades. You have a go and see what you come up with! I wonder what A.I. would come up with.

But physical exercise? Just think about it. Most of us would have been up before breakfast racing around the hills with the dogs fetching the cows to be milked. We would have walked (which included much running hither and thither) or ridden our pushbikes to school. The bikes would have had no gears. They were the ones which the rider really did have to push; push down hard on the pedals to keep the thing moving forward. They are probably not even called pushbikes anymore.

Those pupils with hills to negotiate on their way to school would do their damnest to conquer all of them. Which young country kid would want to lose face by having to admit defeat, dismount his bike and push it up a hill. That's not what a pushbike was for! Luckily there were no steep hills on my way

12. Hop... Two, Three

to school where one would have to get off and push. I never had to admit defeat.

After school our physical activities would continue in one form or another – probably both. There were many times when, with a faint echo of Mum's, 'You boys, stop running around in the house', I would head for the open spaces. Yes, sadly, I would often be caught for my brothers were much older than I, but I would always live to run another day. Yes, they were my brothers but luckily neither had streaks of Cain within him. Later I grew to outpace them.

No, any education which involved 'Hop two three', 'jump two three', or running on the spot would have been treated as a joke and our teacher realised that.

When I run, I want to get somewhere, especially if one, or both of my older brothers had reason to chase me.

'Where did you hide my cigarettes, you cheeky little bugger? When I catch you. I'll show you...'

'If you can catch me!' and off I'd run.

We remained healthy and fit without any organized physical education sessions. My daily activities would have included most of the elements a gym junkie today would pay big bucks for. Thinking about a few:

Skipping. Yes, there were skipping ropes hanging up in the play shed (I even had one at home myself as a young chap). Individual skipping was a popular lunchtime activity, perhaps more so for the girls than for the boys. Then running in and skipping a twirling rope, twirled by a couple of enthusiastic friends eager to catch one's slow ankles. Most were more than happy to swing the rope at pepper speed and even happier to accelerate into hot pepper. So, most of my skipping was done at school, but not as Phys Ed, simply as fun at lunch time.

Walking machine. You must be kidding! We spent our lives walking (or running) without the help of an expensive machine. We were the ones moving and not the ground beneath our feet.

Stress relief. Sitting for a couple of hours each day, squeezing cows' tits and relaxing against her warm flank would stave off the worst of demons.

Weightlifting. Life on a mixed farm before technology lightened many loads, was a life of lifting. You wanted something moved, you had to lift it – buckets of milk, horse collars, bales of hay, tins of potatoes, forks of hay, to name just a few.

Rope climbing. We had trees, and all those containing birds' nests were fair game. Veritable monkeys we could be if there were desirable eggs waiting to be stolen. Climbing was a normal activity for a country kid, sometimes with a rope, usually without.

Yes, there were activities aplenty waiting to be performed with no instructors, no standards to reach (except that of one's dad if it involved work around the farm!), or even aim for. It was all part of life.

The absence of a Phys Ed slot in the daily school program did not mean that we would spend the whole day at school without doing anything physical.

'Did you run around in the classroom?' One may be asked.

'Heaven forbid! No way. Maybe kids do that today, but we wouldn't think of doing that. Old Jack wouldn't tolerate behaviour like that.'

12. Hop... Two, Three

'How did you get the exercise?'

'Out on the school grounds at morning recess and lunch time.'

'When did you eat?'

'Eat?'

'Yes, your lunch and morning tea.'

'We ate at morning recess. We were hungry by then. Most of us would eat breakfast very early and so by morning recess we would be very hungry. We'd eat our lunch then.'

'And at lunch time?'

'There would be no food left to eat, so we would have all that time to play games.'

'All of you?'

'Yes. I can't think of anyone who didn't want to play something or another. Wait a minute. There was Dopey Danny.'

'Dopey Danny?'

'Yes. His name was Daniel. He would always be 'too busy' and we could never get him to join us in our sporting activities outside the classroom. Spent most of the lunchtime walking around the schoolgrounds looking for trapdoor spiders.'

'Wasn't that dangerous?'

'No, not if you're careful.'

'But it is a funny thing to do, isn't it?'

'Not for Dopey Danny it wasn't.'

'I suppose he went on to become an arachnologist or something like that?'

'No, nothing like that. He left school as soon as he could and worked on the family farm.'

At lunchtime Mr Barton would go home for lunch (he lived

adjacent to the school) and the rest of us older kids would race down to the school paddock for a game of rounders. There was no such thing as a school oval, but the school yard was flat and level, occasionally mowed, so it was easily used as a rounders field.

'How many are down here today?' Mal would ask.

'Ten, Mal,' someone would call out after a quick check.

'That means we can have six on each side,' Mal decides after a little mental adding up and taking away (arithmetic wasn't one of Mal's strong subjects). 'What?' as he heard a comment from one of the kids.

'Only five, Mal.'

'Who asked you, Charlie? Now pipe down or you won't get picked.'

And without more interruptions, Noel and Mal, self-appointed captains for the day – for most days actually, for they were two of the biggest kids at school – would begin selecting their team members, taking it in turns. Previously they had drawn straws – usually paspalum for that was readily available on the school grounds – to see who would have first pick.

This whole process of picking teams was somewhat pointless for the sporting ability of every kid at school was well known and they would inevitably be picked in the same order. Who picked first was the only variable and that depended on the paspalum grass.

There could also be some variation depending on what Charlie or Melvyn had kept over from their morning recess lunch box. The picking would have hardly begun when Charlie, occasionally Melvyn, would have pushed to the front of the group. Here he would be jumping up and down, waving his right arm in the air (yes, the right one, for we were all right-handed then), and shouting out, 'Pick me, Noel. Pick me!'

'I'll have you next, Sam,' said Noel ignoring Charlie.

'Noel, pick me, pick me. I've kept some biscuits from morning recess.'

Noel paused and looked at Charlie. 'Biscuits? What sort are they Charlie?'

'Jam drops, Noel. Mum made them on Saturday. I've got three left.'

'Jam drops,' repeated Noel screwing up his nose and shaking his head slightly. Then looking around he continued pointing at a shy little fellow standing at the edge of the group, 'Dessie.'

Finally, Charlie was the last chosen. Chosen was probably not the correct word.

'Come on then, Charlie,' sighed Mal, or Noel depending who had drawn the shortest straw at the beginning, 'You'll have to be on my team.'

That decided, the game could begin if...

'Charlie did you bring the bat and ball?'

'No, Noel, they're still lying beside the play shed where you put them yesterday.'

The sporting equipment needed for our schoolyard rounders was very elementary to say the least. The bat, a broom stick (i.e. the handle detached – one shouldn't ask how – from the sweeping part of a broom) and a tennis ball too old and shiny to be used on the court were the only two essentials. The bases were smooth basalt stones dragged up from the creek. They would be left lying in situ on the rounders field, until Mal and Noel got sick of rounders and a different lunchtime game became popular.

'How are we going to play without a bat and ball, you silly galoot. Now race up and get them.'

'Yes, Noel.' Off Charlie would scamper as fast as his legs could carry him. Charlie, himself, would agree that this was not very fast.

With the necessary preliminaries attended to, the game could begin. It was never a carefree, fun-in-the-park type game, but a serious, competitive affair as if the ashes themselves depended on the outcome. One team would win and the other lose, but like the farming families of which all team members were a part, the losers would hope that it would rain tomorrow.

Or next time they would be picked in the winning team.

Interschool sporting events?

Nothing much to remember here and I also needed a prompt to get me trying to remember any. This was recently provided by an old golfing companion whom I knew from baby days. Went to church together back then, sitting on our mothers' knees.

'Remember this?' he asked, showing me a faded black and white photo.

It was a shot of sundry kids lined up in two rows and very hard to recognize anyone.

'No,' I replied as I looked more closely after taking it to where there was more light. Then I recognized myself at the end of one of the lines and my mate near the end of the other.

'School cricket teams.'

By then I had worked that out. I think the cricket bats and

12. Hop... Two, Three

one of the kids wearing batting pads gave it away. We were in different rows (teams) for Clarrie went to Lower Tent Hill State Primary School and I went to Upper Tent Hill State Primary School.

Clarrie explained. 'That's when your cricket team came down to play us.'

Our cricket team? With fewer than thirty kids going to the school nearly every boy there would have been in the team.

'No, I still can't remember. Who won?'

'Wouldn't have a clue,' Clarrie had to admit.

Which got me thinking about sporting visits to other schools. I then remembered playing tennis against some other schools in the district, going to Junction View and Ma Ma Creek on another occasion. Whether we won or lost the matches I have no idea.

The next thing that came to mind was going to district athletic carnivals at Laidley and wearing brown and green ribbons, our school's designated colours. Which makes sense with the brown for the fertile Lockyer Valley soil and green for the crops.

I still have some certificates from way back then – 1949 and 1950 (that is way back!). One was for coming first in high jump in 1949. Then there is one for coming second in broad jump (it doesn't say how long I jumped). A third one is for being third in high jump in 1950. It seems that I had reached my peak in 1949 when I won. The outstanding one, however, is a first in the State Championships. Here the boys intermediate relay team from the Lockyer District, of which I was a member, conquered all. I remember that Peter, another kid from Upper Tent Hill, was in that team as well. All that running around the hills chasing wild plums, birds' eggs and delinquent cows paid off.

But ah! Alas. The school will not see glory days like that again. It closed some years ago for lack of pupil numbers.

13.

Where there's smoke . . .

SO THERE WE WERE, two naughty – on this occasion I would have to admit that to be the case, but then hasten to add that this was not usually a word used to describe us – nine-year-olds sitting behind the chook pen in Uncle Augie's back yard. We could have been ten-year-olds; perhaps even eight-year-olds. I don't remember exactly.

I must point out that when we started talking about this particular episode dredged up from our young years, it all seemed a little hazy to me, but Col was most adamant that it did take place. Then after much detailed description, which had to be based on real facts one would think, I could picture everything so clearly. Or was it the power of suggestion, Col's suggestion? He can be very convincing if he chooses to be, and I am loath to admit to a fading memory. I am always amazed how some people can remember such fine details from so long ago.

'Three Threes,' he claimed, 'don't you remember?'

'Three Threes? That's nine. We all know that,' and I laughed, trying to make light of my lack of recollection of what he was talking about. 'But no, nothing about cigarettes or smoking comes to mind.'

'In a green packet.'

'Nope, I can't see it.'

'A small packet. It was only a packet of ten.'

'And how did we, or should I say you, get hold of a packet of ten cigarettes?' I asked with a frown on my face. Three threes (that's NINE) in a packet of TEN was another of his 'facts' which caused me to be suspicious of his story.

No, Col assured me, he didn't pinch it from Singh's corner store. I did believe him about this, for stealing was something we just did not do. We both had been well drilled in the ten commandments at Sunday School, and the seventh one said quite emphatically – or was it the sixth? –Thou shalt not steal. I'm sure at that time we could have continued quoting from our well-memorised catechism:

What does this mean? We should fear and love God that we may not take our neighbour's money or goods, or get them by false ware or dealing, but help him to improve and protect his property and business.

I can still recite that one (It is the seventh, by the way. I've checked) and the nine others, all with their explanations as per the catechism. With some I would need a certain amount of prompting.

'So where did you get that packet of . . .What brand were they?'

'Three Threes. Don't you remember the ads in the paper?'

13. Where there's smoke ...

'No, why on earth should I remember cigarette ads in the newspaper? I only ever looked at the comic strips and the cricket pictures and stories.'

'*Smoke **Threes** for a week; You may find them the cigarette of a lifetime.* That's what the ad said. And it's not a full packet. There are only four and a half in it.'

'And a half? Did you pick it up off the streets somewhere?'

That wasn't a silly question for I knew Col collected empty cigarette packets and tobacco tins as a hobby. He lived in town at that time, and it was easy for him to build up his collection. He would simply scour those places where he knew smokers (men mainly) gathered – sports grounds, pubs, saleyards, garages – and add to his collection by picking up the discarded empty packets. He had also told me that quite often there was still a cigarette or two, and sometimes even more, in a discarded packet.

I lived out on the farm, infrequently went to town, and so building up such a collection wasn't possible for me. My older brother did smoke, but he kept to the same brand – Capstan, if my memory serves me correctly – and so he would not be a good source of empty packets. The whole point of a collection is to collect *different* varieties. Along the nearby roads? Yes, empty packets were tossed out of passing cars, but these were few and far between (packets, that is, not cars). And to tell the truth I had no desire to have such a hobby. I had my birds' egg collection to keep me busy.

And Father was a pipe smoker. His wasn't a fancy pipe but an unadorned, straight-stemmed model. Not like Uncle Otto's from up the road. He had one with a bent stem. I would look at the two and often wonder if it altered the smoking experience and enjoyment to have the smoke go around the curved stem instead of simply along a straight one. Probably not. It could be purely a matter of aesthetics or a preference for shape. The pipe aficionado may be able to confirm this and enlighten us further, but I am not he.

I can still see Father and Uncle Otto on an autumn Sunday afternoon sitting on our front veranda in the sun having a quiet pipe together. Not a lot of conversation. Neither were great talkers, only ever saying what was necessary. They were enjoying each other's company, with the odd observation and comment, in a gentle haze of sweet-smelling aromas.

It was right and proper that they were able to savour their pipe in such a relaxed manner for it could be seen as the final chapter of a set routine, a sort of pipe-smoking ceremony. Let me explain.

First the pipe itself had to be prepared. The lower part of the stem was detached from the bowl section and thoroughly cleaned. Pipe cleaners were pushed backward and forward through the tube collecting the nicotine and other waste product which had been deposited when last used. Mum did have a thing about dirty pipe cleaners which were left lying where they shouldn't have been, and Father was generally careful about where he left them. Then with a pocketknife which was part of the smoking paraphernalia, the bowl of the pipe would be reamed clean.

Next, or previously, the tobacco had to be cut from a plug with the same knife. Pipe tobacco could be purchased ready prepared in tins but both Father and Uncle Otto preferred smoking plug tobacco (I think now that cost could have been an important factor in their making this choice). After the

13. Where there's smoke ...

cut-off strips of tobacco were thoroughly kneaded in the palm of the hand by vigorously twisting and rubbing, only then would it be carefully, firmly placed into the bowl of the pipe.

A lighted match would be applied, and a few deep puffs would ensure that the tobacco was alight. Special waxed matches were generally used for these would burn for a longer time ensuring that the tobacco was well alight and one's fingers were not burnt. With the tobacco slowly smouldering the smoker could relax in his chair and savour the fruits of his preparation.

In this era – I am speaking about the middle of the twentieth century – the pathway to a smoky future was certainly open to all. This was a time when there were no pressures, medical or societal, demanding abstinence. Smoking was part of life. I had, before me as a child growing up, two examples of how I could choose to become a smoker: my father with his pipe or my older brother smoking cigarettes. My early attempts were directed towards the cigarette. It is no wonder that cigarette smoking was the preferred option, especially using ready-made cigarettes. It avoided all that preparation which seemed necessary for the pipe to operate successfully.

It was generally assumed that everyone (speaking mainly about boys, for it was considered unladylike by many) would give smoking a go. It wasn't likely that I would follow in my father's footsteps and be a pipe smoker while still a kid in short pants. Ten-year-olds smoking a pipe could only be seen in a Dicken's novel. It was the cigarette waiting to embrace me.

In spite of the general acceptance, it was primarily regarded as an adult pastime. It was assumed that children did not smoke but they should wait until adulthood. When was that?

The age at which children became adults seemed somewhat fluid depending mainly, so it seemed to me, on individual parent's decision. When you left school was another indicator. This placed the line in the middle of the low teens, for the majority left school after reaching the compulsory school age – fourteen when I was a kid. All this was not a great issue as far as I was concerned because I planned to continue my education well past the compulsory age. And I felt no great urge to start smoking.

The result was that I didn't rush into smoking. That said, I did not isolate myself completely from the habit. It was always there waiting for me. Clem, from up the road, and I had, on several occasions tried smoking; tried our version of smoking.

We were not able to come by any real cigarettes or actual tobacco which could be made into roll-your-owns. Short of pinching our brothers' supplies, something which was fraught with dangers if we were caught, and Clem had learnt the seventh commandment at Sunday School too. Nevertheless, there were forces enticing me down the pathway to addiction.

Clem was enthusiastic and keen to give it a go, so we had to look for some suitable substitute for genuine tobacco. We could not pick up the used butts of our older brothers. They were very fire conscious and when they had finished a cigarette did not just throw the dumpers away willy-nilly. They would throw them onto the ground and grind them round and around with their feet to make sure they were completely extinguished. This mixed any remaining usable (for us) tobacco irretrievably into the dirt.

So what alternatives could we lay our hands on?

The corn crop was in tassel and the corncobs were swelling

13. Where there's smoke...

with smooth fibers protruding from their tips. Inventive young souls that we were, we saw the potential here to indulge in a little subterfuge-styled smoking. We chose that corncob silk as a possible substitute for Golden Flake Virginia Fine Cut or Capstan Ready Rubbed. Or was it we picked up this possibility from some of the older, wiser, more experienced kids at school (Cousin Noel would have been a definite possibility). After all schools are not just for teachin' readin' and writin' and 'rithmetic.

So up the hill to father's promising crop of corn where we selected samples of silky strands from the tops of the cobs. With a little bit of imagination, it really did look like fine cut tobacco. We rubbed it thoroughly in our hands, aping what our fathers and older brothers did, an action which, we understood, brought out the true flavour.

Then the next problem arose. We had no special formulated cigarette papers in which to roll our own 'tobacco'. These purpose-produced bits of paper which came in small packets, were impregnated with various additives which control the burning rate. We were unaware of these scientific details and assumed any available paper would do the trick. After all the local newspapers served very well as toilet paper so why not double as cigarette paper as well?

We had to choose between The Toowoomba Chronicle and the QT (Queensland Times, published in Ipswich). Clem's dad would get The Chronicle but my dad favoured the QT for some reason. I never did understand, for most of our larger-town dealings were with Toowoomba. We also had The Sunday Mail delivered but the women seemed to favour that for the lavatory, finer texture perhaps, and it was all accounted for.

We chose the QT, for we were doing the experimental smoking behind the hay shed on our farm. We also wisely chose an older edition for we didn't want Father asking why his paper had square, or rectangular, holes cut in it. Then with Mum's good scissors we cut out a number of rectangular shapes with the width approximating the length of a cigarette and of sufficient length to get a few good rolls. I remember being very proud of the neatly rolled homemade cigarettes which Clem and I had produced. They were a little longer and fatter than ready-made ones, but this might add to our pleasure.

We borrowed a box of matches – Redheads – from the kitchen cupboard. Mum had a wood stove at that time and there was always a supply of matches ready at hand.

We each took a cigarette, smiled a sort of congratulatory smile, and prepared to enjoy the fruits of our labours. I placed my 'QT Corn Silk' between my lips, struck a match and lit the end. It caught alight with a small flame burning the excess paper not containing 'tobacco'. I breathed in, hoping to have the fire engage the corn silk and start the smoking process. Nothing happened, no smoke, no taste. I breathed out ready to breathe in again but all of a sudden the whole thing burst into flame, burning my cheeks and singeing my eyebrows. I grabbed and spat at the same time, finally sending the life-threatening object flying.

It landed on some dry grass which immediately caught fire. Clem was laughing his head off but had enough wits about him to stamp out the fire.

'You should have seen yourself.'

'Seen myself? Lucky my eyes weren't burnt out of my head!'

'At least I put your fire out.' Clem was right with that. After all that was to be expected for he was a country boy who knew the dangers of fire.

'Yes, thank Goodness. We could really have got into trouble. Can you smell my eyebrows burning?'

'No, they're not burning.'

'I wonder will the same thing happen when you try yours?'

'Don't be stupid. No way am I going to light mine up. I don't really feel like a cigarette now, anyway.'

'Maybe we need greener silk?'

'Not me. I've had enough smoking for today. Let's go over to our hayshed and see if we can get the pigeon eggs there.'

This minor mishap did not stop us searching for some other tobacco substitute at a later date. We tried pepperina tree bark, lucerne leaves and probably a lot of other things which I've forgotten about. Oh, yes! We also tried horse manure. That was taking things a bit far, some may think, but I got the idea from my brother. He was trying out a new brand of cigarette which he said was cheaper than his usual brand.

'Heavens, I won't be buying them again!' I heard him say to Alan next door. 'They taste like horse shit!'

I had no idea how he knew what horse shit, as he put it, tasted like. Working with draught horses as he did back then, and having his own riding horse, he would have often mixed with horse manure, but as for tasting it?'

This gave me the idea, so Clem and I tried some roll-your-own horse manure cigarettes. After a few puffs, we tossed them away.

'Yuck! They taste just like horse shit,' was Clem's reaction.

With all those earlier abortive attempts at smoking behind me, one would have thought that the time had arrived to say enough is enough. No, in my boyish ignorance the best was still to come. I was now ready for the big time. Yes, I was now ready for ready-made cigarettes with real tobacco. That time had arrived with town-wise cousin Col, half a packet of squashed Three Threes and me behind the chook pen.

At an early stage of our escapade, it was obvious to me that Collie had handled cigarettes before. The finesse with which he extracted his from the packet, the practiced subtlety used to align the cigarette correctly before placing it between his lips, showed quite clearly that here was no amateur. Col's 'Threes' was soon protruding boldly under his glasses ready to receive the fiery match and be sacrificed in the interest of our further education.

I was still trying to fish out one of those remaining in the crumpled box, each of which was mortally squashed. I finally seized hold of one and pulled it out. I looked at it lying limply in my hand. I stood there looking pensively, sadly, perhaps a little reverently, somewhat like Abraham, I could imagine, who was about to put a knife to his son, Isaac, and sacrifice him on a pile of burning stones.

I sniffed. There was this smell of tobacco – perhaps a little dry and dusty – not the sweet perfume of the smoke from Father's pipe. I concentrated and soon had the cigarette gripped between my lips. Even more than that. I had shoved it so far into my mouth that I could bite firmly onto its end. I waited.

Collie in the meantime had taken out a match and struck it alight and was holding it at the end of his cigarette, vigorously sucking in. Soon its end was aglow and Col's head had disappeared in a cloud of smoke.

13. Where there's smoke . . .

'Here,' he coughed, 'take a match and light yours up.'

'OK,' I mumbled through tightly closed lips, which were desperately holding a fag in place. With a quiet prayer (I now realise it was probably made to Vulcan) I struck a match and held it upright.

'Well, don't just stand there like a dumb chook. Light the fag.'

I slowly brought the burning match towards where I thought the end of the cigarette should be. It made no contact. I had stopped before I had reached its end. I was probably subconsciously remembering the time I singed my eyebrows.

'Hurry up! Light the thing.'

'Auch!' I yelled as the match burnt my fingers, flickered out and then fell to the ground.

'Here, try again,' Col mumbled through the cigarette balanced precariously between his lips. He took another match out of the box and handed them both to me.

I had put my fingers up to my mouth wanting to suck them where they were burnt. I realised too late that with a cigarette there, that was not possible. I ended up sucking on a cigarette which was pushed even more out of alignment. I suffered in silence. Then I steeled myself to have another go at lighting the cigarette.

I succeeded. I sucked and a stream of hot, nicotine-ladened – as I now understand – smoke billowed into my mouth, down my trachea heading for all the bronchioles and alveoli of my lungs. I hastily breathed out and a rush of smoke invaded my nares.

I sniffed and coughed and spluttered but unwisely did not stop there. I took another draw. What a foolish thing to do!

The result was similar but the coughing more intense, enough to frighten the chooks off their nests. I am sure Aunty Hilda wondered why there were no eggs to collect the next day. No home-made sponge cake for Collie and Uncle Augie that weekend. I spat and coughed and spat again.

'Schh! Dad will hear us and wonder what we're up to,' warned Col.

Alas! Too late!

'What are you two young mischief-makers up to there?' Had a good nose for sniffing out mischief did Col's dad, my Uncle August.

Yes, we were caught red-handed. The remainder of Col's cigarettes were confiscated and both of us led inside by the earlobes. It was probably then that I decided to give up smoking; or should I say I decided not to take up smoking. Since that day, smoking (of anything – horseshit to hashish) for me has been a 'no, thank you'.

Luckily those few inhalations behind the chook house seemed to have no serious and long-lasting damage. Later in life those same lungs which I had repeatedly tried to poison, were able to propel me across the finishing line of many 440-yard tortures.

14.

Birds' Eggs

I WAS BALANCED FIFTEEN precarious metres, or more, above the grass, sticks and stones lying on the ground below. It was probably more, but that was immaterial, for a fall of fifteen metres would cause as much pain and break as many bones as a fall of twenty. Back then, it would have been so many *feet* above mother earth and that would have made it seem even higher, and even more dangerous.

'Can you feel them? How many are there?' My mate, Clem, looking up from the ground at the foot of the tree, wanted to know my progress.

I dared not reply. The least little movement on my part, yes, even moving my lips to speak, may have upset my equilibrium, and sent me tumbling out of the tree and into hospital. God forbid, that should happen! I had told all the other kids what a good tree-climber I was, and I really had to live up to my reputation. Mum, too, would have been very annoyed. Only later, when I was less foolhardy, did I realise that much more than my reputation could have been damaged.

On this occasion I was lying, fully extended, on a slender branch high up in an iron bark tree. My feet were wrapped around the fork where the frail branch supporting me left its thicker, bigger brother. My left hand gripped another quite small twig barely in reach above my shoulder. This gave me some balance, some sense of safety. My right arm? It was fully extended in front of me so that the hand was just able to feel into a crow's nest.

Clem and I were determined to add a crow's egg to our collection. They were hard to come by for crows had a habit of building their nests high up in tall trees, out on small branches. This crafty positioning presented difficulties for us young kids: strict orders about climbing high trees from parents and the danger of falling and hurting oneself being the main ones.

We were aware of this nest being built – it was just up the hill from where I lived, in an area we called the forest. Now seeing that one of the birds was always sitting on the nest it was time to act.

14. Birds' Eggs

One Saturday morning we made our way across to the forest determined to get the eggs. I had drawn the short straw and had to do the climbing. Clem's job was to hold the makeshift ladder (it was actually a fallen bough from a nearby tree) which I shinned up to allow me to reach the first branch of the towering iron bark. Then he stood and watched, giving instructions which were neither necessary nor appreciated. He idly waited for his share of the spoils to be delivered.

I had to climb my way up starting with my whole self (in reality only my arms and legs) wrapped around the trunk, which in this case posed few problems. This technique was bread and butter to a regular climber. A slight slip at one stage resulted in grazed legs and a painful testicle. These things happen when climbing. As the height of the tree increased, the size of the branches decreased until the one selected by the crows barely supported my weight. But except for a little soreness between my legs, slightly scratched arms and grazed inner thighs from the rough bark of the tree (they are not called iron bark for nothing) my goal was within reach without serious mishap.

I lay recovering my breath and wondering how I would reverse along the thin branch without toppling off. From experience I knew it was often more difficult coming down from the top of a high tree than climbing up. But that was getting ahead of myself. First things, first. The eggs.

To make matters worse, mum and dad crow were becoming more and more agitated. They knew that something evil was afoot. I'm sure they were deciding how best to deal with this uninvited quadrupedal invader, human as well, which had slithered along the branch to invade their nest. Their initial swooping runs at me were merely the beginning of a more concerted attack. I tried to ignore them, but it was difficult. Their swoops were coming nearer and nearer to my bare head. I couldn't shoo them away for both my hands were fully occupied.

I took a deep breath. To work. I had to find out how many eggs I would have to deal with. I put my hand into their nest and felt three eggs. I had one between my thumb and forefinger when 'Snap! Snap!' the crow's beak was mighty close. I jumped in fright (no, not out of the tree luckily), and my hand reacted by closing too tightly on the egg in its grip.

'Bugger!' I cried out.

'What?' shouted Clem in response.

'I just broke one of the eggs.'

'You what?'

'I just broke one of the eggs. The crow snapped so close to my ear that it gave me a heck of a fright. I had an egg in my fingers, and I crushed it.'

'That was a stupid thing to do! How many more are there?' Clem asked.

'I think there's two. And it's alright for you standing down there on the ground. You don't have two angry crows dive-bombing you.'

'Two. That's OK then; that's one each. But try not to break them after we've gone to so much trouble.'

'We,' I thought, but chose not to say anything. It was important that I concentrate and make sure I secured those remaining two in one piece. Ignoring the complaints of the two crows I grabbed the two eggs, one a little slimy from the contents of the broken one, firmly in my hand.

14. Birds' Eggs

But where was I going to put them as I climbed down the tree? I would need both hands free to make my way down safely, so I couldn't hold them in my hands; not even one hand. In one of my pockets? That's the usual place but ... The front pocket of my shirt was pressed tightly against a branch. No room to put them there. Pant's pockets? Again, both were tightly closed clinging closely to my bum cheeks. Besides, in pants pockets was never a safe place to hold eggs while sliding down a tree trunk.

Only one option remained. Put them in my mouth. It was often done that way by us band of egg collectors. Sure, it was the cause of a little laughter when other kids heard about it: 'Straight out of the bird's bum and into your mouth!'

That's what I did. I popped them into my mouth and started the descent. Things were going well. I had resisted answering Clem's questions which he kept firing up at me. I was pleased in a way that there were only two left for that's about all my mouth would safely hold. Crows are big birds and the size of their eggs confirm this. I was halfway down the tree, eggs safely intact in my mouth when I put my foot on a small, dry branch which I had used on the way up. Oops! It broke. I must have put more weight on it on the way down. My reaction was to grab around the tree more tightly to stop falling. My head jerked forward, and my cheek hit against the bark of the iron bark. Auch!

Bugger! Bugger! Both eggs were crunched. I was left with a mouthful of eggshells and interiors, in this case with half incubated embryos.

I spat it all out. I don't remember any real taste. Only the taste of defeat.

I got down safely. Well, with grazed cheeks, arms and inner thighs. 'Also', as Clem never stopped telling everyone, 'with squashed balls and broken eggs'. He was quite annoyed standing there completely undamaged and having done nothing to help.

We still did not have any crow's eggs. Somewhat disappointed at that time? Sure, but as we both were well aware, things do not always go according to plan. Hopefully there would be another time. There were always plenty of crows flying around and they must have come from somewhere.

Both Clem, who as you know, lived just up the hill from me, and I, had a collection of birds' eggs. We weren't the only ones who collected birds' eggs as a hobby. When I think about it, the majority of young boys in the district had a collection and each one of us thought his own was the best. Most of us were pretty competitive and strived for the best collection; the one with the most varieties. We were always on the lookout for that extra hard-to-come-by egg, the rarer, the harder to locate, the more difficult to reach, which would give a collection the edge.

Taking a few risks like those involved in reaching nests high in trees or sneaking into a hard-to-get-on-with farmer's property, was seen as par for the course. No serious accidents were ever reported; only wounded pride and shattered eggos.

Mention our hobby in some circles today and one would be lucky to escape with only a verbal battering, as though the actions of a number of small boys a few generations ago could bring a species to the brink of extinction. Sure, bird numbers may have declined in recent decades but there are other reasons for that.

14. Birds' Eggs

No, I am talking about the time before the mass introduction of chemicals and insecticides into the farming environment. This was the time when sky and trees were full of our feathered friends. Our collecting was seen as an interesting pastime which cost nothing (not like stamp collecting) and where the objects of interest were readily at hand. We regarded it as avian birth control. That's not really the case. Those thoughts never entered our heads. Protest groups marching to 'Save the sparrow' and 'Love our Lorikeets' did not exist.

So we felt no pangs of conscious, for abundant birdlife was a fact of life. Starlings would crowd the power lines from one post to the next. Finches of one sort or another – zebras, double-bars, red-beaks – would have all the small bushes and shrubs crammed full of their nests. Pigeons would plague each and every hayshed in the district. Pesky sparrows were everywhere (they still are). Crows, magpies, butcherbirds, wrens, mickeys and happy families made the fields and forests alive with their sounds. And they all built nests, laid eggs (the female of the species, that is) and provided interest and adventure for us country boys.

A basic collection was easy to acquire. On the mere walk, or bike ride, or horse ride to school one could see enough nests which in egg-laying season would provide enough variety for the beginner to get up and running. It would be a simple matter of robbing (Ouch! That doesn't sound a very nice word) the easily reached nests and getting the eggs home in one piece. Perhaps that wasn't always as easy as it sounds for small eggs are very fragile and easily broken, especially when your 'friend' gives your pocket a whack when he knows there are eggs in it.

Once home safely, one of mum's sewing needles easily makes

a small hole in the top and bottom of the egg and the stuff inside can easily be blown out. But easy does it, especially with small, fragile eggs. Blow too hard and yuck! The whole egg bursts asunder with goo all over the kitchen (or loungeroom, or veranda) floor which would bring more than a frown from Mum. Successfully emptied, the shell soon dries out and the collection has begun. That is, after it has been decided how to store and display them.

'Hey Mum, where's the cotton wool?' My sister was shouting to Mum.

'It should be in the medicine cabinet where it's supposed to be.'

'Where in the medicine cabinet?'

'Heaven's above! You shouldn't need a search party to find something in there.'

'Well, you come and look. I can't see it anywhere.'

Of all the luck! Just when I had nicked the cotton wool to line another shoe box for my new bantam eggs I got from Noreen at school, Sis decided to clean the cut in her toe. It appeared that she needed Dettol and cotton wool. In the middle of artistically arranging my new bantam eggs, with slightly varying colours, I was interrupted.

'Glen!' a duet of feminine voices reached me in the washhouse where there was a cupboard in which I was allowed to store my collection. They were not allowed inside the house for some could pong slightly until they dried out properly. It seemed that they had decided who was to blame for the missing cotton wool.

A second 'Glen' reached me, louder this time.

'I'm out here in the washhouse. What's wrong?'

14. Birds' Eggs

'Have you swiped the cotton wool again?' my sister asked. 'And not put it back where it belongs?'

'I'm in the middle of using some.' I dared not give them the impression that I had just used it all up. I should have known that this stalling tactic was just prolonging the inevitable.

'Well, you should stop what you're doing and bring it back now. I need it to clean my foot.'

I slowly walked back into the house and into the bathroom where the medicine cabinet was screwed onto the wall beside the wash basin.

'Well, have you got it?' I was greeted with a rather aggressive question.

'There wasn't much left on the roll and I had to use it all to line another box for my new bantam eggs. You know, the ones Noreen gave me at school.'

'You what?'

'Just told you. Used it all for my bantam eggs.'

Mum stepped into the conversation before it had a chance to escalate. 'I seem to be buying cotton wool every time I go to town. You will have to try to do with less, or use something else to line your boxes,' Mum directed to me, and then turning to Sis she added, 'We'll find a rag somewhere to clean off your cut. That should do the trick.'

I took the opportunity to quickly leave the bathroom, the house and the immediate vicinity. I walked down to the orchard to see how the persimmons were coming on.

As kids living on the land, we soon learnt the habits and idiosyncrasies of all members of the bird world. We knew their names (well, the local names, or the names we knew them by.

I still have arguments with city-bred people about the name of a bird), their calls, their habitat, their nesting habits. This latter was important for the egg collector. You had to know where the bird might build the nest to lay the eggs.

See a peewee scratching about in the mud – in my case near the chooks' water trough – you knew it was getting mud for a nest. All you had to do was follow it when it flew off and she, or he, would take you to their building site. And a willy-wag-tail's nest was often nearby in the same tree. Same with turtle doves and top-knot pigeons. Follow them when they have a few straws in their mouth, and they will lead you straight to their nest.

Knowing nesting habits did not always mean that we could easily locate a specific nest. And there were surprises.

Most varieties of parrots would nest in hollow branches of trees usually high up. But not always. One pair of rosellas I knew had their nest in a hollow round post at the entrance of our farm. Every year they would be there. Their eggs were safe from me and Clem for we already had rosella eggs. We would only ever collect one good example of each type of bird. Once we had that, their nests were safe from us robber collectors. Our interest would then be in watching them raise their young.

On one occasion we were standing at the base of an old iron bark looking up at a pair of galahs checking out the space in a dry, broken-off branch. It was quite high in a tree that had no low branches, making it unlikely their nest would be in any danger from us. This scenario represented one of the frustrations of egg collecting: knowing that an egg you want is up there in the tree but beyond your reach. No access to cherry-pickers back then.

14. Birds' Eggs

All of a sudden. Swoosh!

'What the heck!' Clem jumped, almost knocking me onto my backside.

I had heard a flapping of wings and an unearthly screeching as a flash of colour flew off from below our feet.

'That was a lorikeet,' I suggested.

'Maybe,' Clem replied, 'but where the hell did it come from?'

We looked down. There was a hole in the base of the tree. To our knowledge it was unlikely for a parrot such as a lorikeet to nest so close to the ground.

'It must have come out of that hole there. Maybe it has its nest there. Put your hand in and see if you can feel anything,' I said.

'You gotta be kidding,' Clem was quick to reply. 'You never know what might be in there.'

No way would he investigate. He probably was thinking of the time he put his hand in a hole along the creek bank which we thought was a kingfisher's nest. He touched something smooth and slippery and wriggling. He had pulled his hand out so quickly that he fell back into the creek. To cap it all off he got into trouble from his mum for coming home from school in wet clothes.

I was intrigued so I knelt down and shoved my arm into the hole at the base of the tree. In and in it went as far as I could maneuver it. Nothing. The nest must have been further up than I could reach. A few days later, out of curiosity, I went back to the tree. I gave it a whack with a stick and a lorikeet came screeching out. It was probably as scared as we were when it gave us that fright. At that, I left her in peace.

Although we thought we were experts in the nesting habits

of birds there were often surprises. It was often not so easy to locate the actual nest which we knew must be in the vicinity. This could require a bit of serious surveillance or diligent searching to track down a nest we knew must be somewhere. This applied to a couple of basically ground-dwelling species quite common where we lived.

Quails and plovers, although so different in appearance, used a similar strategy to keep us egg hunters from finding their nests. If the truth be known, they probably had developed their strategy long before we human egg stealers came along. Before us, there would have been four-legged, or winged, or slithering-along-with-no-legs egg stealers. Both quails and plovers would construct no elaborate nest but lay their eggs on the ground. The plover would choose the open fields with no camouflage or protection whereas the quail would hide in the grassy patches.

'Just sit and watch.' You may suggest.

Yes, that is one strategy, but the protective parents seemed to be aware of one's presence no matter how stealthy one might approach. As long as they knew you were in the vicinity (and, as I said, they always seemed to know) they would not linger near the nest. On the contrary, they would try to attract your attention away from the nest's location.

Quails would frequent the grassy strips along fence lines and as they were ground birds would spend all their time doing whatever quails do in the cover of the grass. If they were startled and had to break cover, you could be well assured that they would not fly out from anywhere near their nest. Luck and/or a thorough search was the only way to break their defences.

14. Birds' Eggs

But they were usually no match for a couple of boys who had nothing else to do (their parents would have disagreed with this) than sit and watch, or slowly search in the thick grass until they had success.

Yes, all that effort, all that danger, all that time searching the wooded hillsides looking for a butcherbird's nest, or a leatherhead's nest or whatever else we were lacking, came to an end when I went off to boarding school. There my excess energies were directed towards other pursuits. And my collection of shoeboxes lined with cotton wool and full of treasured eggs often obtained with much difficulty? What became of it? I don't really remember. Mum probably needed the cupboard space in the washhouse for other purposes and quietly disposed of my eggceptional collection.

Just another one of those unanswered questions from my childhood.

15.

Terry

TERRY WAS MY OLDER brother, some ten years my senior. He was baptised Terence; Terence Lester, but everyone called him Terry. In many minds, I imagine, and no doubt often in reality, a ten-year-older brother is someone who ignores you for the first few years of your life, avoids you when you start making your presence felt in the family and then bosses you around when you're old enough to do the jobs he is supposed to do.

That was not the case with Terry. I remember him as a kind, caring person.

If I wanted to know something – the meaning of a word, the capital city of a country which I'd heard mentioned on the news, stuff like that – I would go to him. If he didn't know the answer, together we would set about solving the problem. There was no 'What do you want to know that for?' or 'If you want to know that so badly go and find it out for yourself' which, I heard from my friends at school, are common responses from older siblings. And yes, unfortunately,

15. Terry

I've been given responses like that myself. But never from Terry. Well, not that I can remember.

It was Terry who was always happy to have a hit with me on the tennis court or bowl a few overs to me (again on the tennis court), although he wasn't really interested in sporting activities. He was more interested in things like drawing and music. I often wished that I could draw maps for school as well as he could, or colour in copies of a pineapple from a Golden Circle tin for my art class which he had no trouble doing.

He had an interest in leather work, a sort of hobby of his, but also making straps and things which were needed for the horses. He had a work area set up on a table on the side veranda. I would often help him when he was making something like a small purse, a belt or a cover for a book, or maybe repair in a bridle strap. I could poke holes in the leather with an awl providing he marked where I was to make the holes. I didn't have the strength to sew the leather pieces together but I could wax the thread Terry used. Never would he tell me (well, hardly never) to 'Get out of my way, and stop being such a nuisance'.

And everyone would comment how musical he was. Did he learn the piano as a young lad? I'm not sure. He probably did for Sis did. She became quite proficient – to my ears – at playing hit songs from sheet music or hymns from the big black church hymnal. Terry's musical notes which linger in my mind, do not come from the piano. No, from a much smaller source. I can still see him sitting on the couch in the dining-room strumming his ukulele and singing some of the top ten hits of the time.

Zip-a-dee-doo-da.
Zip-a-dee-ay.
My oh my, what a wonderful day.

Sioux City Sue was another favourite.

And then there were various homemade versions of *She'll be coming round the mountain when she comes.* One favourite version was:

She'll be riding on my Triumph when she comes.
She'll be riding on my Triumph when she comes.
She'll be riding on my Triumph; riding on my Triumph.
She'll be riding on my Triumph when she comes.

This was a favourite because Terry owned a motor bike: a Triumph. That was its make. And he loved this new motorbike.

15. Terry

He got it mainly to go to work. Not to go to work on the farm for he didn't stay working on the farm like my other brother, Ron. Some people liked being farmers, and others didn't. Terry didn't. He had a job working at the butter factory in Grantham about six miles away.

His friend, Louis, from over Ropeley way, also worked at the butter factory. He also had a motorbike, but I have no idea what make. He would call in at our place of a morning and he and Terry would ride off to work together. I can visualise their route. It went down the road past the local pub, up over Mietzel's Hill to Ma Ma Creek where Bob Higgins had his blacksmith shop, through Winwell and then over a few more hills to the village of Grantham.

Here they would ride past Wally and Ivy's place. Wally also worked at the local butter factory. He probably put in a good word for Terry and helped him get the job there for he was our neighbour before he married Ivy and moved into Grantham. Then it was past Gilbert and Lena's residence. They were my Mum's uncle and aunt which would make them my great uncle and great aunt, but I just called them Uncle and Aunty. A few doors up on the other side of the street was Uncle Alf and Aunty Freda. Freda was one of Mum's younger sisters which made them my real uncle and aunt.

They are all dead and gone now. The houses they lived in have also gone, either washed away in the great Grantham flood of 2011 or moved up the hill to a flood-free zone.

After passing these relatives and friends they would ride under the railway bridge to the factory. The factory building is still there but hasn't made butter for many decades. It has been refurbished for other uses.

And I was so proud of my big brother's motor bike and loved to sit on it when it was stationary, going 'Brumm! Brumm!' imagining I was speeding down the road. Mind you, I had difficulty reaching the handlebars while sitting on the driver's seat and my feet remained dangling above the footrests for the seat was so wide and my seven-year-old bum could not straddle it, making my legs shorter than they were.

This was probably the extent of my motorbike riding experiences. I have never owned a motorbike; never even ridden on one!

Terry kept his pride and joy spotlessly clean. I was always keen to help but he claimed that I was more a hindrance than a help when he was washing and polishing. This would happen every Saturday morning, out on the side lawn. Here he would park the bike, fetch a bucket of water (no hoses then!), a cake of soap and a few rags and the ceremony would begin: an initial washing and then a very careful cleaning and polishing. I would help, making the black petrol-tank shine, rubbing the nickel-plated exhaust pipe and other bits and pieces until they were dazzling and ensuring that the black tyres were free of any dust and dirt. Then they would contrast so splendidly with the white wheel rims.

Mum would shake her head at my enthusiasm. 'If you spent as much time washing your feet as you do with polishing that bike, your sheets mightn't be so dirty for me to wash!'

It was a Wednesday morning (I really don't remember it being a Wednesday, but I have checked that out for the purpose of this story), and Clem and I were halfway up the hill behind our house looking for wild plum bushes.

15. Terry

We each had a stick in our hand and would belt the grass in front of us as we walked along. This was to frighten away any snakes which might be lurking there. We also used them to poke under the bushes and shrubs looking for those elusive wild plums.

Wednesday? What was the reason for not being at school? That's easy to answer. It was still the Christmas holidays, still two weeks before school started – 16th January 1946. I remember that date!

From where we were on the hill we could look out across the valley: straight ahead (west) to the creek down near the pub; down the valley (north) along the long lane towards Gatton; south, not so far for Bill Weier's hill hindered the view in that direction. East was to our back. So, in two and a half directions in which we looked, the fertile Tent Hill valley opened up with its patchwork of fields, at this time of year mainly green, black and yellowish-brown (lucerne patches, fallow land and the remains of pumpkin crops).

We were watching a vehicle coming up the long lane from Gatton. At the corner it turned and came up heading to our place, and then turned in towards the house.

'That's a police car,' Clem suddenly said after looking at it for some time. 'What on earth is it doing here at your place?'

I shook my head. 'No idea. Maybe he's lost and looking for someone else.'

We considered going down to see what the police wanted but knew that Mum and Father would tell us to stay outside and not be so nosey. We went on chasing the snakes and searching for plums.

'There's another car coming up your road,' Clem noted after

we had reached the top of the hill and were looking around the valley to see what was happening.

'That's Pastor Koehler's car, isn't it?' I replied.

Clem nodded.

'But he visited us on Monday. What's he doing back again?'

This time our curiosity really did get the better of us and we headed off down the hill to the house. We barged into the living-room.

'Hey, Mum, what's the pastor . . .?'

We stopped in our tracks. Mum was sitting on one of the dining-room chairs sobbing into her hands with father standing beside her with a hand on her shoulder.

Who said mums don't cry?

The police sergeant had brought news that Terry had been killed in a bike accident.

Living on a farm one soon becomes aware that dying is part and parcel of life. A cow would become sick and die, in spite of a possible visit by a vet, which I might add, was a rare occasion for us at that time. A horse might break a leg and would have to be 'put down'. Then I remember my pet dog, Bluey (he was also the farm's working dog), being bitten by a snake and dying. Sure, I was sad for a while but then Spot, or another Bluey would arrive to claim my affection.

I remember one newly arrived dog who got the name of Dummy. As a cattle dog he was always on the lookout for something to herd and always came off second best when chasing the cream truck or one of the infrequent cars on our road. Dummy was short for 'You stupid dumb bastard. I can see why Harry was so keen to get rid of you!' which father shouted

15. Terry

at him when he seemed to lack those basic instincts which make a blue cattle dog a cattle dog. I was fond of him too, but he eventually got knocked over and killed while chasing a car.

Attending the funeral of a relative, a friend, a fellow church member or even an identity in the district may have prepared other members of my family somewhat for Terry's death, but not me. As a young child I do not remember going to a funeral. The country funerals were held during the week when I would have been at school. At that time my close relatives were still all alive and so it was not necessary for me to miss school to attend one of their funerals.

All the events leading up to Terence's funeral were new and upsetting to me, a bewildered seven-year-old.

We were soon made aware of how the accident happened. His friend, Louis, had not ridden to work with Terry that morning. When Terry had not turned up at work by starting time he jumped on his bike and rode back to see what was holding him up. There were no mobile phones in those days. Alas! There, under the railway bridge, a mere 200 metres from the factory, Louis came across the Triumph lying on the road and Terry lying dead in the grass on the side of the road. Apparently, the bike had slipped over on the sandy surface of the road and Terry had fallen off, hitting his head on a rock.

He would have been killed instantly.

Details of what happened can explain to some extent how the accident occurred but do not explain why it should have happened. There seems to be no answers to the 'whys' of tragedies. Philosophers and theologians have attempted explanations but can any of these lessen the grief felt by those impacted by the death of a loved one?

Our home became flooded with the hundreds of black-edged sympathy cards and letters of condolence which arrived in the mail. It became more and more apparent just how deeply the short life of this young man had touched the lives of people throughout the whole district.

Over the next days a continual stream of visitors kept arriving to show their respect and give support to our family. I don't believe our kitchen and food pantry ever held as many supplies of cake and biscuits as it did during those day when Terry was lying in the coffin in our lounge room.

His lying there was a discomforting presence which struck me every time I walked through the room to my bedroom. This prompted an unfortunate moment which I have never forgotten.

'What a funny smell in there!' I innocently remarked to the family while we were having a meal together.

This comment was met with shocked silence. Father got up, took me by the ear and pulled me into the next room where he gave me a hard whack on the backside. This was not like him.

'Do not speak like that!'

I can now appreciate that it was his grief directing his actions towards me, but at that time I felt it differently.

The whole district attended his funeral service at the Ropeley Lutheran Church and his burial at the church cemetery. The crowded church and the equal number of mourners standing outside illustrated so clearly how Terry's unexpected death brought sadness and deep grief to so many, not only his immediate family. The shared grief of those attending the funeral surely did lessen the impact on my family. However, it is the comfort afforded by one's Christian belief in a future resurrection and a life with one's God that does most to lessen grief and keep the memory of a loved one alive.

Terry was seventeen years old.

16.

In the Onion Patch

FATHER PROBABLY DELIVERED THE bad news while we were all sitting around the kitchen table having morning tea. It was quite unusual for the whole family to be having morning tea together in the kitchen. On normal occasions Mum would take a billy of tea and a ration of cake and biscuits down to the men working on the farm somewhere while Sis and I would grab something whenever we had the opportunity (or opportunities, in my case).

This, however, was a rainy day and 'the men', i.e. Father and my older brother, Ron, were doing jobs in the sheds or the workshop next to the house: mending horse harness, sharpening tools, servicing machinery, stuff like that. There was never an idle moment for the farmer, rain or hail; but especially sunshine. At the appropriate time on rainy days they drifted inside for a cup of tea and something to eat. Mum would soon have a variety of home-baked cake and biscuits on the table.

This day, Father, I remember, came up onto the veranda with a wet corn bag over his shoulders – the farmers' substitute for a raincoat (no Drizabone in those days!). So it was clear to us that he must have been out in the weather.

He told us that he had returned from the onion patch.

'It can't wait any longer,' he exclaimed to no one in particular as we were sitting around the table. We all looked at him, waiting for him to continue and let us know what was bothering him. He just picked up his cup of tea and began blowing gently across the top to cool it. He would often tip the tea into the saucer so that it cooled more quickly; but he didn't on this occasion.

Finally, Mum asked, 'What can't wait?'

Father took a sip of his tea, found it still too hot and put the cup down on the table. We didn't use saucers at morning tea time for that would have created more washing up. That would also explain why he blew his tea to cool it rather than putting it in a saucer.

Eventually he replied, 'Chipping the onions. We need to get into it right away.'

'Oh, no!' I blurted out knowing what that meant. Father's 'we' included me, and it was school holidays when I was expected to help on the farm.

'We have to get straight at it. Wait any longer and there will be all hell to pay. All going well we should be able to start tomorrow. This weak rain front will have moved through by then and the soil will be moist and easy to chip.'

That's something about my father. He had a fair idea of what the weather might be doing. Like all farmers who generally spent their whole working life at the mercy of the weather, he was a bush meteorologist, quite at home throwing around words such as fronts, storms, westerly wind, dry spells, bloody hot days as well as those at the other end of the spectrum where the temperature could freeze the balls off a brass monkey.

'And the westerly wind?' asked Ron. 'It's not going to be very pleasant down on the flat with the wind blowing.'

'Yes, we can expect some cool air coming up from the south. That's usually the case with this type of front. Might need to start off with a coat on.'

With that the matter was closed. The prospect of chilly gusts sweeping across the countryside would not stop a family foray into the farm's field of weeds and struggling onion plants.

Young onion plants are delicate little things barely able to fend for themselves and in an open field where a whole range of botanical monsters are vying for dominance they do not fare well. They are also very slow growers and this places them at a distinct disadvantage for the weeds could soon smother them. They need help and their competitors need to be cut down to size. In those distant days before weedisides (Zero, Roundup etc.) the deadly hoe was employed, wielded by human hand.

Father had inspected his crop on this rainy day. This was not at all surprising for there is nothing he enjoys more than mooching around the farm on rainy days with a corn bag over his shoulders making a sort of tour of inspection. This day the unacceptable activity among the little onion plants caught his attention.

There were little strands of wild couch grass just waiting for the opportunity to send out their runners and take over.

The less-than-welcome stems of wild onion weed were taking refuge close beside their distant cousins.

16. In the Onion Patch

Throughout the field little green dots of what appeared to be thousands of pigweed babies were emerging from the soil where previously their mothers had spread their seed.

Little thistles, burrs, flannel weed and myriads of other varieties were watching, keen to avail themselves of father's fertile field. Some scientific boffin may have ascribed them Latin-sounding names in years gone by but to my dad and me they were simply weeds. And they had to be stopped.

Came the morning and with it the wind; a chilly morning indeed. In spite of this, the four of us – Father, Ron Merle and me – strode (Father and Ron), ambled (Merle) and dawdled (me) down to the onion patch.

You would think that the weeds would be more comfortable resting snugly beneath the surface; but no. There they were before us, seemingly without a worry in the world. How little they knew! Soon the axe would fall. A hoe really: an onion hoe.

Forward into battle determined (well, not all of us so much) to stop the little onion plants, each merely a tender three-inch-long shoot, from being overrun and suffocated by a weedy army of invaders.

To work: Father and Ron where the weeds were the thickest and Merle and me where there were fewer of the enemy. Young onions are fragile plants with an undeveloped root system. They are easily uprooted and one has to tread lightly when walking amongst them, and chip carefully. Luckily (actually, by design) the onion hoe has a narrow blade so one can accurately target an offending weed without chipping out an onion plant by mistake.

Mind you, sometimes this would happen, particularly if a healthy weed was growing very close to a struggling onion.

The safe method – the one adopted by my father – was to bend over and pull the weed out gently with one's fingers not disturbing the soil near the onion plant too much. But I often didn't follow this edict. I was confident of my accuracy and a little too cavalier in my approach and would bring the hoe down with deadly force. I must admit there were often casualties – killed by own fire, so to speak. Luckily Father would seldom check our work and when dealing with five acres of onions one or two (or more) inaccurate chips had little, if any effect on the final harvest.

To make this experience of chipping onions even more unpleasant was the fact that I didn't even like onions. Sure, I liked the taste of the rich, onion gravy which Mum would make to go with the pork chops but I would painstakingly pick out the onion pieces and leave them on the side of my plate. I could not enjoy the texture and raw taste of the onion's flesh. But I had to put that culinary dislike out of my mind. This wasn't difficult to do for the thin, struggling plant was a far cry from the firm bulb into which it would eventually grow.

Now with three rows of onions lined up in front of me and my hoe dangerously active, work was progressing. Three rows? Yes. You see onions are planted in rows about a foot (30centimetres) apart, and the idea was to weed the space on either side of a single row.

The rows ahead seemed to fade off into infinity. Here's me, just a small chap, barely past the three times tables at school, wondering how I would ever get to the end. But horror, I then realised: when I got to the end I would have to turn around and come back along the next three rows.

Three up, three back. Three up, three back. This would be

the rhythm of the day.

I looked up and another reality struck me. The westerly wind was blowing straight into my face.

I turned my face around to avoid the wind and saw Father coming up behind me, shoving with his hoe and kicking with his foot.

I turned to Sis. 'What's Father doing?'

'He's making sure you're doing a good job.'

'A good job? I'm just chipping out these weeds.' I looked puzzled.

'You'll see,' she gloated.

Father soon caught up to me.

'How's it going?' he asked.

'All right, I suppose.' I was non-committal. I didn't want to tell him that I didn't like chipping onions (he probably knew that already) and that I would rather be roaming around the hills looking for birds' nests.

'Look here a minute,' he said. 'See that?' as he poked a weed which I had just dislodged from where it was growing.

'Yes. That's a weed, isn't it?' I didn't know what he was getting at.

'Yes,' he assured me, 'that is a weed and it will still be a weed in a week's time.'

'Yeah, but a dead one.'

'That's the point, Son. It probably won't be dead. Its roots are still half in the ground and with this moist soil it will recover and keep growing.'

'Hardy little buggers.' I thought I joked.

Father was not amused.

'No, you must make sure that you are chipping them out

completely. Otherwise you are wasting your time here and could well be somewhere else.'

I was smart enough not to suggest some of other thing which I could be doing and merely murmured, 'Yeah, I'll go more carefully and not try keeping up with Sis.'

'Good lad. If we all chip in as a family we'll have this finished in no time!'

I looked across at five acres of family fun.

Father went back to his weedier workplace and Sis and I chipped along in silence except for the occasional warble of delight coming from a member of a magpie family which was following us hoping that we might disturb something for its mid-morning snack.

All of a sudden a 'What on earth are you doing?' came from my sister.

'Chipping,' was my innocent reply.

'Why are you going back over what you've already done?'

'I'm not.'

'Yes, you are. You're facing that way.'

'I'm walking backwards but chipping forwards.'

'You're what?'

'The westerly wind was blowing straight in my face, so I turned around and I'm chipping as I walk backwards.'

Sis didn't seem to be impressed. 'That's the most stupid idea... And you'll trample on all the onions, or trip over on your backside and squash them all.'

I took no notice of her assessment of my idea and slowly kept on chipping with the wind on my back.

Eventually Sis asked, 'Does that really keep the wind out of your face?'

16. In the Onion Patch

'Yes. Why don't you try it and see.'

She frowned for a moment and then, 'I'll give it a go for a while.'

She turned around and soon got the idea. Then she noticed that she was stepping very close to the onions. She looked around to see if the rows of onions had shifted. They hadn't, but somehow her feet became tangled and she fell down on her backside right on the row of onions.

I laughed.

She quickly got up, her pride probably more bruised than the onion plants.

'Shut up your laughing, will you! I said it was a stupid idea!'

But we all chipped on and no doubt finished weeding the whole crop. I don't actually remember my last blow with the onion hoe.

The crop grew and prospered, eventually maturing enough to be harvested – picked is the technical term. As I remember I had to help a little with the picking, ending up with smelly hands, teary eyes and snipped fingertips. But that's another story.

17.

Milking Time

I REMEMBER MUM SAYING to me after she had retired into Gatton leaving my brother, Ron, and his family out on the farm, 'I don't understand why they don't keep a cow instead of running into town every time they need a bottle of milk.'

'I'll tell you why, Mum.' I came to my brother's rescue.

'Well?'

'They don't want to be tied down to milking a cow every morning and evening just for the sake of a few bottles of milk.'

That touched a slightly discordant note in my mother's memory. She knew exactly what I was getting at and so she grunted a barely audible 'Yeh' (or something similar) and suggested we go out back to her vegetable garden where we could dig up a few carrots to take back home with me. She never did give up trying to get me to eat carrots even though I wasn't wearing glasses.

Being tied down was the main complaint of farmers, and their wives, who had a herd of milking cows no matter how small or large. The blighters had to be milked morning and

17. Milking Time

evening, seven days a week, fifty-two weeks of the year. That meant that on a small family farm – and where I lived, most were that in those days – it was difficult to get away for a break, for a holiday.

Mum didn't actually spend much time in the cow bails milking once we children had grown up (not so much 'grown up' as being old enough to milk a cow). She would stay inside getting on with her household chores. At milking time this meant preparing breakfast and tea for the rest of us. But she was aware of the annual holidays which her non-farming relatives would tell her about and knew that the cows were mainly to blame for our lack of a week or two down the coast.

And I spent my childhood on such a mixed farm, the family farm, where the cows had to be milked morning and evening. As a result, I grew up not knowing about annual holidays and from a young age I had to help with the milking. That's just how it was. For me it all added up to many hours spent in the cow bails; many hours with my head pressed firmly against a cow's flank; many hours squeezing cows' tits. No wonder there are memories of these hours etched indelibly into my brain, but no memories of holidays.

Mention cows being milked today and most will see an image of cows lined up being milked by these cups over their teats which are sucking the milk out and sending it all to a central large vat. Sure, there were milking machines around when I was a kid, but only those dairy farmers with large herds had them. Only they could afford them. At our place it was a hands-on activity.

There was no getting out of it. The sparrows were up, the sun was up, and I, together with my sister and brothers, had to be up too. 'Rise and shine, Sleepy-head!' was my early morning wake-up call. I dare not stay lying in bed.

What about on bleak, rainy mornings? Yes, the cows had to be milked. Who cared if one had to struggle through rain and puddles and end up being soaking wet. Tomorrow the sun would be shining, and the clothes would dry. Well, if not tomorrow then the day after.

On cold, frosty mornings? Yes, the cows' udders would be pinching and in need of relief. At least I had an old coat to put on – a hand-me-down from one of my brothers, no doubt – to protect from the cold. On these mornings it was good to put my head deep into the cows' flanks for warmth. And I would also be hoping for one, or more, of the cows to do her morning 'mess', as Mum called it, in the cow yard. I would relish warming up my cold feet by tramping up and down in a heap of steaming cow crap. Momentarily it was good and comforting, but this posed another problem before breakfast.

'And Glen,' Mum was speaking after I had finished my morning chores, 'don't think about coming inside with all that cow mess on your feet. Go out to the washhouse and clean yourself up.'

Then, without argument, it was out to the washhouse to wash my feet clean in cold water for there was no hot and cold running water out there. Not in the whole house, I might add.

Generally, things went well at milking time. It was all routine and nothing to get worked up about. We kids would get on with our milking knowing which cows we each had to milk. Father, at times, could become a little annoyed. He was, everyone would agree, a mild man, not one given to using bad language. Occasionally, however, when things were not going smoothly, and when he was particularly annoyed, a 'bloody' could slip into his expressions. It can happen to the best of us, and yes, it had happened to him in the cow yard.

We had two cows, Maisie and Star, who were very skilled at annoying him. One habit of theirs was especially annoying. Let me explain.

These two delinquents would mostly hang out together. On a hot day, if one was in the shade of a particular tree the other would be there beside her. Should Maisie be grazing the far end of the paddock, Star would also be there. Thirsty? They would drink at the water trough together. Time to relax and ruminate? Their mouths would be chewing in perfect harmony. Clearly, they were in some kind of bovine relationship which we had difficulty understanding. But then, if you think about it, cows often behave like overgrown lemmings.

But none of these things particularly annoyed Father. That was fairly normal milking-cow behaviour. Their bad habit, the one that really got under his skin, was being missing at milking time.

Our small herd of some twenty head was milked twice a day: in the early (too blinking early for us kids) morning and again in the late afternoon. The milkers were aware of this schedule and would usually make their way to the milking bails at the right time. Occasionally they would be somewhat remiss and would have to be rounded up. Yes, by me and the dog. All that was part and parcel of milking and caused no great concern.

But often Maisie and Star would be missing when the rest of the herd was patiently waiting. Their absence really irked my father. Why it got to him so much I could never work out for I was the one who had to go looking for them every time.

'Glen, those bloody cows are missing again.'

'That's two times already this week,' I replied innocently.

'I know you can count to two. Just go and find the bloody things.'

'Ah! Can't Sis go this time?'

'No, it's your job.'

'But it's so cold this morning. There's a heavy frost, you know.'

'Of course I'm aware of that. I can see. Running up the hill might warm you up a bit. Off you go, then!'

'Oh, it's not fair,' I moaned again. Then shouting, 'Bluey! Bluey!' with steaming breath, I moved out of the confines of the relatively warm milking bails (it was actually very cold in there as well) into the frost of a breaking dawn.

Bluey? He was our blue cattle dog, a necessary addition on all mixed/dairy farms. No, not a very imaginative name like, say, Anthony or Toodles, but he was no pampered lapdog. Bluey was a working dog. All the farms in the district had a blue cattle dog to help with the animals. Most called their dog Bluey. If I could have shouted loudly enough I would have had half a dozen dogs helping me track down our pair of late-comers.

With Bluey jumping along in front and me tramping through the frosty grass we headed for the hill.

At night the cows were free to graze, or sleep, or whatever, on a hill behind our house. It was called a 'hill' by all of us but to a young lad sent out to locate two cows lurking up there somewhere it was a Mount Everest. The missing cows could be anywhere on the hill. Should I go to the right, to the left or to the top? On the other hand, they may have decided to have

17. Milking Time

an early drink and be down at the trough on the flat. This is where Bluey would show his worth. He seemed to know instinctively where they would be.

He would bound off in one direction carving a route through the long, frosty grass. I would follow, confident that this would lead me to the two wayward beasts. It almost seemed as though Bluey had some inbred instinct designed specifically to counter the actions, indeed even the intentions of refractory bovines.

'Why bother following him? Why not let him fetch the cows by himself?' you may ask.

A good question, but ... Bluey could not resist chasing hares, a close relative of the rabbit. If he were to spy a hare or two out for an early morning nibble – and this was their preferred nibbling time – he would suppress his natural instincts, forget the cows, ignore his duty towards me, and go tearing off after those hares. I had to be there to keep him on task.

Job done, we would arrive back at the cow bails with the two recalcitrants; Bluey wet all over with dew, but happy; I with my shorts wet halfway up to my backside from running through the long, wet grass, my feet two degrees off freezing and not particularly joyful.

Bluey would have a few laps of fresh milk from his tin which was kept beside the milking shed. Then he would stretch out and relax. I would begin milking my quota of cows, happy in a way to be able to put my head into the warm flank of the cow I was milking, and probably sitting a little closer than usual for warmth.

Cows ain't just cows, you know, and it's not just because they come in a variety of colours. True, if one were to have a pure, say, Jersey herd, it would be difficult for the layperson to distinguish a Maisie from a Star. However, each cow does have her own personality and – this was very important to me – each had her own milking difficulty index. In other words, some were easy to milk, others difficult and others even more difficult.

As the youngest with the smallest hands and weakest wrists I was allotted the quiet old dears with tits so pliant (vets would probably have a technical term for this) that the least squeeze would send a stream of milk into the bucket. It generally took the older, stronger and more experienced milkers (i.e. my dad and older brothers) to handle the younger, perkier animals.

So, seated on a stool – it was a short block of iron bark – with half a corn-bag doubled over to make it softer and more comfortable, the process began. As I remember, this doubled-over corn-bag didn't really do its job for the seat was still hard and uncomfortable. The milk was directed into a galvanised bucket either held off the floor between one's knees or simply standing on the concrete below the udder. The latter was not the preferred option for if the cow became a little restless, annoyed by something or another, she could kick out and the bucket would go flying, spilling the warm, white milk all over the floor.

Father was never pleased if this happened. He would make some adverse comment often with 'bloody' in it somewhere. Perhaps he was seeing the loss of income this implied, a halfpenny, maybe, but probably not. Just concerned that something had gone awry in his milking shed.

The farm cat saw this as an opportunity to dart under the

17. Milking Time

cow and have a few quick licks before it was kicked out of the way or the milk became too dry. I would take the opportunity to give her a few squirts of milk between the eyes, or wherever on her body they ended up.

The cat really was one who stayed clear of most of the farm activities. She would appear on the scene from time to time but generally kept to herself somewhere. Puss, to my knowledge, had never seen the reaction of tardy cows when Bluey had given them a nip to hurry them along. Seeing them jump and kick and start running would have set the alarm bells ringing and suggested that she stay clear of their flying hooves. Even aware of the danger lurking under the cow, a lick of warm milk was enough incentive for her to venture so close to the cow's hooves. She never came to any harm.

Our cat would always be hanging around at milking-time hoping for a nourishing drink. And yes, she would always get what she wanted. If Bluey was napping, she would sneak a number of laps from his tin. This would never happen if the dog was awake and watching. He was very jealous of what he regarded as HIS tin and would chase the cat off quickly if she came near it. I often wondered why we didn't have a special tin for the cat.

She and I would play a kind of daring game. If she were to come too close to me, I would give her a squirt between the eyes. I considered myself a dead-eyed-dick with a cow's tit. She was aware of this and would stay just out of range, daring me to try and reach her. It would often happen that my milking bail (we each had our own bail for we always milked the same cows and they knew where they were to go when their turn came up) looked more like a combat zone with spilt and lines of drying milk radiating from where the cows' udders would be positioned. But she was a very astute opportunist and would always have her hunger satisfied.

'You milk a cow from the back, don't you?' a city cousin of mine once asked me.

'What do you mean, from the back?'

'Through the back legs.'

'You mean sitting behind the cow and shoving your arms between her back legs?'

'I suppose something like that. That's where the udder is, isn't it?'

'Yes, it is there, but what a silly idea. Where did you get that idea from?'

'Why is it silly? Don't you do that?'

'Just think. If the cow became annoyed and kicked out – and they do from time to time – you would cop it right in the face. And believe me, most cows would react if you approached them like that.'

'Oh!'

'And another thing. If the cow decided to relieve herself – and quite a few do when they are being milked – you'd end up with cow shit and piss all over you.'

'Oh!'

'No, we come in from the side.'

'Oh. No problem there then?'

'There are still problems. Some cows can't stand still, and they keep kicking around. They need to be leg-roped.'

'Leg-roped?'

'Yes, we loop a rope around their near back leg and tie it

tightly to a post behind them. This holds their leg in place, and they can't kick out with it. The bucket stays safe. The milker too.'

That cousin came to stay a few days on one occasion. Naturally he came along in the afternoon to be part of milking-time. He couldn't make it in the morning for he was still asleep when the rest of us were up and away. He wanted a go at milking. All visitors did. It seemed such a rural thing to do. They see us milking and assume that it must be an easy thing to do.

He sat down on my block, and I showed him, then told him, then showed him again exactly what to do. Now it was his turn, his big opportunity. He sat down on the block and squeezed and squeezed. Nothing. He squeezed and grimaced. Nothing. Poor old May, who happened to be his victim, was wondering what was happening back there with her udder. She tried to look around to find out. She couldn't for her head was firmly clamped in the bail. Some more squeezes and pulls interspersed with grunts, and by this time even quiet old May was getting restless. She almost trampled on the neophyte's foot. He finally gave up. City cousin, Tony, couldn't even coax enough milk out of May's udder for a cup of tea.

'A day-old calf could do better than that,' I told him.

'Funny! I couldn't even get a little squirt, and you said she was easy to milk. What must it be like with those who are hard to milk?'

'No. It's not easy, this milking.'

18.

The Creek

THE CREEK BED IS dry, dusty, untidy. Clumps of scrawny grass and rank weeds now struggle for survival where once crystal-clear water flowed. Being blown aimlessly among this weary vegetation are leaves and twigs, dry and brown, brittle and faded olive, searching for those greener, less thirsty times. Stones and pebbles lie scattered around, partly covered by the hot, parched sand. They are dull, lifeless, no longer sparkling in the running water.

There is a rattling in the dead bushes at the bottom of the right-hand bank and a crow's mournful caw comes from a far distance, then another, and another.

I shake my head in disbelief. Then I look up at the blue sky and recite:

I chatter over stony ways
In little sharps and trebles.
I bubble into eddying bays,
I babble on the pebbles.

This is a stanza from a poem (*The Brook*, by Alfred Lord Tennyson) which I learnt many years ago when I was going to the school just up the bank, the left-hand bank, from where I am now standing. At that time, it would have so accurately described this creek here which I would have to paddle through to get to school. Where has that creek disappeared to?

Yes, many decades have passed since Clem and I (and other kids, too) would cross the creek here going to school. We wouldn't always cross it here for there were different ways of going to our school which was about three or four miles upstream from where we lived. We could choose between horse, push-bike (with no gears) or foot. And we could go up the right-hand road, the left-hand road or through the paddocks in the middle. We usually chose to ride our bikes up the left-hand road. Then we would leave our bikes at Uncle Frank's place and walk the last few hundred yards across the creek to the school.

But not always directly to school. Each morning would bring new water to the crossing, for this was when the creek never stopped running. And each morning would bring new adventures to us boys who needed to fill in the hour, or more, before the school bell rang and we had to line up to move into the classroom. This is why we would leave our bikes at Uncle Frank's place. They would only hinder us in our pre-school ramblings.

We could paddle through the knee-deep water throwing stones, making ripples, getting wet. We could walk across the log Frank's boys had put across the creek just down from the crossing, a sort of do-it-yourself bridge. This was used when the creek was flowing a little fuller than usual and wading through water over one's knees was not really an option if one's shorts were to stay dry. It was often an annual task to erect the log bridge because the floods would regularly wash it away. It was adzed slightly level on top, all the more safely to walk on, but slippery on frosty mornings. Toppling-in 'accidents' were known to occur. Pushing a girl in the water off the bridge was an accepted way (to us boys) of showing affection.

I clearly remember one embarrassing episode on this bridge. We had just read a poem in our reader at school entitled, *Horatius Defends the Bridge*. You know the story?

It happened back in ancient Roman times. An enemy force was marching on Rome but needed to cross a bridge over the Tiber River to reach the city. The city leaders decided to destroy the bridge and thus hinder the enemy's advance. Unfortunately, there was not enough time to do this because the enemy had arrived. Horatius and a couple of his mates volunteered to hold up the enemy in the narrow approaches to the bridge and thus give the Roman citizens enough time to destroy the bridge. He and his two companions did hold the enemy at bay until the bridge was at the point of collapse. Horatius' two mates raced to safety with the bridge crumbling beneath them, leaving our hero alone to confront the enemy. The bridge then collapsed. A few deadly thrusts with his sword to confuse the attackers and then in full armour Horatius plunged into the flooded Tiber River and miraculously made it to the safe side. Rome was saved!

What a story to re-enact on the log bridge across our creek, which although at the time not a raging torrent, was running quite full. Those wanting to cross here needed to use the bridge if they didn't want to get their pants wet, or even be washed downstream. I had taken up position on the school end of the bridge with a two-foot-long stick as my trusty sword. Alan and a couple of his mates approached wanting to cross on their way home from school. I held my sword aloft.

'All hail! Be it known that you are forbidden to cross these flooding waters,' I cried.

They stopped and looked at me. 'What did you say?'

'You must not cross the bridge.'

'What rot are you going on with?' Alan asked quite aggressively.

'I am Horatius, and I am defending the bridge from the enemy.'

'That's what you think. You are Nat and about to get your pants wet.'

A couple of Alan's mates laughed and one said to the other, 'Natty is about to wet his pants.'

I ignored them for as Horatius I would not be distracted. 'Defend yourself, enemy of our land,' I shouted as I brandished my weapon.

But Alan grabbed hold of my sword (he was bigger than me) while his mates laughed. Then he threw me and the sword into the water below. Only with difficulty did I avoid being washed into the deep hole downstream.

Alan and his mates just had no appreciation of ancient history.

I arrived home soaking wet from top to bottom, schoolbag as well, which didn't please Mum.

'Have you been fooling around on that log over the creek again?'

18. The Creek

I explained how I was re-enacting an example of Roman bravery.

'What a stupid thing to try to do!'

Mum, like Alan and his companions, showed little appreciation of ancient history.

Or we might just spend time exploring the creekbank. Here, at the crossing, was no long monotonous stretch of creek but holes and shallows where one variation followed the next and these provided endless attraction for us young boys. Cousin Johnny, had his set lines in that gloomy hole just a little upstream with the turtles, platypus and water goannas. He wanted to catch the big eels – and often did. We would check the lines occasionally for we wanted to pull in a big eel too. This was something Johnny didn't like.

'What would you do if there was an eel on the line?'

'How big an eel, Johnny?' Clem might ask.

'Who cares how big. Two foot, three foot, even eighteen inches. You little kids couldn't handle it.'

'Oh, come on, Johnny, we're not kids anymore.' Well, Clem and I were probably eight or nine at that time.

'You couldn't hold a twisting, slimy eel. It would twist my line into all sorts of knots and ruin it. If it was big enough it could even pull you into the creek. That's a deep hole there and you would probably end up drowning. You stay away from my set lines!'

We took no notice and kept checking them from time to time. It was probably lucky for us that we never did have to deal with a big eel at the end of the line and probably get the line all knotted up. Worse still, we would both have received a good kick up the backside from Johnny.

Downstream from the crossing was a large, deep hole where Albert had set up a pump to irrigate his paddocks. One couldn't easily walk along the bank to get there. The lushness with its birds and insects hung far out over the water. Even the accessible parts along the banks involved nettles, tall sticky paspalum, burrs and sharp thistles (because Old So-and-so up the creek further didn't keep his creek paddocks chipped clean of pests and the seeds would wash down), castor-oil bushes, willow trees and numerous other species probably never classified by botanists.

This seemingly impenetrable barrier of ferns and creepers, tea trees and bottle brushes, gums and silky oaks merely presented a challenge to two boys who had the time to explore before school started. Clem and I slashed a path through this dense growth using a short, sturdy stick as a machete.

We were not necessarily heading anywhere but merely living a jungle experience, and perhaps would be able to see more of Albert's pumping hole.

'Shh! What was that? There are probably snakes here.'

'Don't be silly, Clem. Snakes slither silently and we wouldn't hear them. That was a rattling.'

'Well, what was it?'

'Surely you know. Just stop and listen for a moment.'

We stood quietly and soon heard a splash nearby.

'It was a water goanna. There will be others rattling into the water as well, I've no doubt.'

Then suddenly we were through the tangled mass of vegetation to an open corridor where Albert's pump pipe led down to the water. Immediately below us was the murky, still water of this deep hole.

We scrambled along the pipe to the water's edge and looked over the water. A number of dragon flies and other insects were hovering over the water. Dead leaves were drifting around.

'Hey, look!' Clem sounded rather surprised. 'Those leaves are floating upstream.'

'What leaves?' I queried.

'Those there. They are definitely floating up the creek.'

'It's probably the wind blowing them that way.'

'What wind? I can't feel any wind.'

'There would be wind out there in the middle of the creek.'

'How do you know? I can't see any,' replied Clem. He and I would often get into arguments over the simplest of things.

'Yes, you can!'

'You're talking rot. How do you know what I can see?'

'You just told me,' I explained.

'I told you no such thing.'

'You said those leaves were going upstream and so there must have been wind out there blowing them that way.'

'I bet there would be some big eels in here,' Clem changed the subject. 'I wonder if Johnny has ever put his set lines in this hole?'

Without a doubt there would have been days when we would have learnt more going to school (especially along the creek bank) than we did at school.

There was a period (short) when we would go fishing before school. It was great fun until Old Jack nabbed us. The hole just above the crossing, probably six feet deep at that time, had a convenient willow tree overhanging the deep spot. From its branches, which attracted small boys and which could easily be climbed, one could see the cat-fish idly swimming about in the crystal-clear water below. A short length of fishing line cut off from father's line, a baited hook (no lack of worms in the creek bank) and we could position the fish's breakfast right in front of its fins. Tempting, one would think, but mostly we saw how our juicy hook-shaped offerings were ignored. But occasionally not, and this would mean a quick run back to Aunty Annie's place and she would put our fish in her fridge till the afternoon when we were heading home. But Old Jack wondered why we were barely making it to school on time after seeing us riding along the left-hand road an hour and a half previously. Fishing had to stop.

For many kids in the valley the creek doubled as a swimming pool; pools really, for there were numerous deep holes which could be used. Not all were actually used, for some, like Albert's pump hole had steep, heavily vegetated banks which made them difficult to get to. Others, like the one around Ronnie's bend, were murky and mysterious with snags in the bottom which made swimming dangerous. Still another was very deep – none of us kids had ever touched the bottom – and our parents advised us strictly to stay clear of it. Maybe it contained evidence of unsolved crimes.

Our main swimming hole was just down from the Logan place, where a section of the creek was wide, long and deep. Well for us kids it was. The water was fresh, clear and clean – a crystal fountain bubbling into one end and equally cheerful water spilling out the other. Here was the place to be on a hot Saturday afternoon, assuming father didn't have some pressing jobs which had to be done at home.

18. The Creek

The banks were gentle-to-steep sloping but manageable, made of rich, fertile black loam and relatively clear of vegetation.

As the swimming afternoon wore on, these banks became wetter and wetter, slippier and slippier, muddier and muddier. Teams were chosen and mud fights began. The clear, clean home of the resident Jew fish and the slippery eels soon became a muddy pond, being totally abused by a group of shouting, slimy, muddy kids.

This was exercise and fun (not the good, clean type) combined into one activity. No wonder we were always so healthy. The fun could be quite exhausting. Climbing up slippery banks, swimming backwards and forwards, upstream and downstream and dodging mudballs made for tiring times. The mudballs which contained small stones, grit and rotting vegetation held well together and made for firm ammunition pieces which were quite painful when thrown by a strong arm. At the end of the day, we often went home with bruises, scratches and sore eyes; but very happy.

I am standing where the log bridge and fish used to be many decades ago. Looking downstream, I see that Albert's pump hole has disappeared. Upstream, the fishing hole is now sand and stones. The eels have disappeared. The school has closed.

The road remains. And the memories.

19.

Bringing in the Hay

HERE IN THE LUCERNE paddock it was quiet. This silence struck us as soon as we came out of the forest with its noisy birds.

Forest? Now don't get the idea that there was a vast area of trees and sundry vegetation on our farm. No way. Our 'forest', attractive in its own unkempt way, was a small area – perhaps three or four acres – which had not been cleared of its natural vegetation: tall iron-barks and gum trees towering over a collection of smaller shrubs and bushes. Ronnie had planted a few pine trees to add to the variety and fill in the blank spaces.

Yes, in there it had been noisy, in a nice sort of way, but out on the open paddock all was quiet. One could look back at a patchy-green curtain, a leafy sound barrier, and it seemed as though the forest was intent on keeping those sounds to itself, selfishly, locked in like some precious heirloom.

But those noisy tree lovers were enticed out onto the open lucerne paddock, enticed by the snacks sheltering beneath the heaps of hay lying there. They know from experience of previous cuttings, that when Father and Ronnie lift a heap off the ground onto the wagon, the insect life sheltering there will be exposed. There will be a scurrying and a scattering of the bugs and insects, the crickets and beetles. This is easy pickings for the sharp eyes and swift beaks of the visitors from behind the green curtain: the magpies, butcherbirds, pee-wees and kookaburras. In their haste to claim their share, and taste this smorgasbord of treats, they have forgotten to bring their songs. Silence now surrounds them; a silence interspersed by the clicking of hungry beaks.

Even the willy-wagtails and starlings come and join in the feasting.

Where are those field birds which normally call the lucerne patch home – the quails and the larks? The quails had previously scurried off into the safety of the long grass along the fence lines. When the sound of the lucerne cutter being pulled by two large Clydesdales was bearing down on them they quickly made their exit. They will return when all this disturbance leaves their home territory.

The larks might be seen if one were to look skywards. They would be up there somewhere, surveying all these activities from on high. Reminds me of a stanza from Shelly's poem *To a Skylark*. We learnt some of the verses in school.

Higher still and higher
From the earth thou springest.
Like a cloud of fire
The blue deep thou wingest.
And singing still dost soar, and soaring ever singest.

They also will return when their fields look safer.

From home we came through our forest to get to the lucerne paddock, along a winding track which dodged in and out among the trees. Our forest, on the side of a sandy hill, was not like the patch of native vegetation remaining behind Uncle Harry's place. The 'scrub' they called it. There the trees and bushes were growing so closely together that it was difficult to walk in, let alone drive a wagon through. This patch of scrub was at the bottom of a little gully running down from the hills and Cousin Col claimed it was so lush there because of the soakage. He was probably right on this occasion.

The birds had sung as we slowly made our way through our sparse forest with the hay wagon, and this made our forest seem so alive.

The hay wagon? Yes, a **hay** wagon and not the old German wagon which was used to shift all manner of goods and produce around the farm (years before, it also transported produce to the train station in Gatton). This was a purpose-built vehicle, made specifically to cart hay. It was basically a large platform on wheels. With a little care and a lot of stamping down (that's where I came in) a large load of hay could be stacked on it. Reaching to the sky? Hardly, only as high as Father and Ronnie could throw a fork full of hay.

Now here we are, on a hot summer's day, in the hay paddock. A few days ago, the lucerne had been mowed. When it had dried sufficiently, the crop had been raked into windrows. Yesterday Father had spent the morning heaping the lucerne into small piles ready to be loaded onto the wagon – the hay wagon – and taken home for storage in the hay shed.

These heaps were in neat lines – Father was a stickler for

19. Bringing in the Hay

neatness and symmetry – so that Bessy and Emma (the two Clydesdales) could pull the wagon along between them. Then Father on one side and Ronnie on the other, would fork the heaps of hay up onto the wagon as it moved along.

Occasionally Emma might wander a little off line so that she could quickly grab a mouthful of lucerne from one of the heaps which came too close. The ultimate opportunist was our Emma. Father, a kind soul at heart, would tolerate this misdemeanor a couple of times but should it happen a third time Emma would be told quite emphatically that enough was enough.

My job was on the wagon, making sure that the hay was evenly distributed, that the sides of the load were growing straight upwards and to see to it that the straw was firmly tramped down to ensure a well-knit-together load, one that couldn't easily slide off on the way home.

Believe me, I was kept very busy in this job for Father (all the time) and Ronnie (when he had a mind to) were very hard workers and the piles of hay kept coming at me from left and right.

'Come on. Get a move on!' Big brothers can be quite inconsiderate.

'I'm going as fast as I can.'

'Well, you need to go faster.'

'Fair go, Ronnie. There's two of you throwing the stuff up at me and only one of me.'

'That's why you need to go twice as fast,' returned Ron, showing that he was quite at home with ratios.

'And you're almost twice as old as I am.'

'What's that got to do with it? You're not old enough to handle a hay fork.'

I was good at doing sums at school and couldn't agree with Ron's logic. I made a plea.

'Don't keep throwing the hay up in the same place so that I have to spread it around. It would help if I didn't have to waste time moving your stuff around to fill in the low spots.'

'What? You want me to do your work for you?'

'Father throws his up in different places so I don't have to spend so much time spreading it around.'

'So? It's the horses that are the trouble.'

The logic in that escaped me too.

But eventually the hay was piled up as high as it would go. Well, as high as Father and Ronnie could comfortably throw a forkful of hay. I was always proud how I kept the sides going up so straight. No chance of the load toppling off no matter how high it went or how bumpy the track to travel.

Then the slow trip home with Father walking in front of the horses and me still on top, comfortably nestled in the hay, being rocked almost to sleep by the gentle swaying of the load. Almost, I say, for young boys don't sleep during the day. I could have been a world away with only the odd creak from the well-loaded wagon and the crunching of the steel-rimmed wheels on the gravelly track, interrupting the silence.

The forest too, had grown quiet with some of the birds still scratching for more insects out in the hay paddock. And the others? Who knows. Perhaps having a nap.

And soon we would be at the shed, with the trip home seemingly shorter than the one going to fetch the hay. And it probably was, for the horses knew they were heading home and so walked that little bit faster, even pulling a heavy wagon.

Ronnie would be waiting for us at the hayshed having taken a shortcut home, walking through a couple of the neighbour's paddocks. Home, but the job was not yet completed. The hay had to be loaded off into the shed, there to await its fate: stored to feed the stock in times of drought; baled and sold to farmers wanting fodder; or cut up into chaff to be sent off to the produce dealers.

And the hay wagon? It would be off back down through the forest to collect another load or, if the paddock had been cleared, then parked under the pepperina tree beside the hay shed until next time the lucerne was mowed and the hay needed to be brought in.

20.

Tennis Anyone?

I GREW UP IN a house with a tennis court in the back yard. Well, not exactly **in** the back yard. It was over the back yard fence.

This statement, that it was over the back yard fence of our farmhouse, would have been questioned by our visitors at that time. 'Back' was the word which would have been in contention. Most would have agreed that 'over the **side** fence' would have been a more accurate description of its exact location. Mind you I can't recall any argument, or even discussion, about the site of the court.

Wherever its precise location in relation to our house, the simple fact was that no one ever had trouble finding the Tent Hill tennis court. It was at Henry Natalier's place.

The confusion which I have introduced above boils down to the everyday use of the house. Architecturally, it did have a front and a back, with a set of fine-looking steps leading up to the front veranda and the front door. But for the life of me I cannot remember any visitor ever coming to that front door.

20. Tennis Anyone?

once was home.

You see, the track from the public road to the house went past this 'front' door and around to the side. It was here that everyone ended up and came into the house through the side door. So, by default, the side became the front. Why, even we who lived in the house, referred to the bedrooms at the side of the house as the 'back bedrooms' (or the children's rooms, or when wanting to be more specific, the boys' room or Sis's room). This clearly distinguished these two rooms from the third bedroom which was the parent's room. Architecturally speaking this room was at the back of the house.

However, the naming of the bedrooms, the orientation of the house, the seldom used 'front' door had little, indeed nothing, to do with the tennis court. You drove off the public road into the house paddock, parked beside the poinciana tree, walked past the entrance to the house (which was the side door as you already know, and not the front door) then past the dairy to the tennis court.

Our court was similar to thousands of others scattered

throughout the rural communities of Australia. Tennis had become a popular social sport with people of all ages who were willing to have a hit. Basically, only two people were needed to have a game, providing a court was available and that could generally be arranged. A court was something that could be built with a little hard work. A site would be selected, often beside the local community hall if one existed, but usually on someone's farm which was centrally located.

Our farm was selected but I never did ask my dad why specifically. It was no more 'centrally located' than any of the neighbours. It was at our place before I came along so I never gave the question any thought. Someone must have made the decision to build it there. Perhaps it was my dad. He enjoyed having a hit.

The result of someone's decision was that I grew up in a house which had a full-sized tennis court just over the side fence (it was actually the back fence as you would have gathered from my discussion above). It was understandable that I had a racquet in my hand from a very young age.

There was a close relationship between our tennis court and the dairying activities on the farm. Dairy cows required milking bails with an attached yard for holding the cows waiting to be milked. In wet weather this could become somewhat smelly and so was better situated a little away from the house. Dairying, which in our case involved selling cream to the local butter factory in Grantham, also needed a small milk separating building in which the separator was situated. This was a small, square building with a peaked roof. Many, now no longer being used for their original purpose, can still be seen throughout the district. These indicate that

20. Tennis Anyone?

here also was once the site of a mixed farm. Our dairy was situated away from the milking bails and closer to the house for convenience.

The tennis court was squeezed between the milking shed (we called it the cow bails) and the dairy (the small peaked-roofed building I have been talking about where the milk was taken to have the cream separated out). The cream was sold and the now creamless milk was fed to the pigs. They were housed some distance away from the house in the other direction. We shall not go there just now.

But to get back to the tennis court squeezed between these two vital establishments on the farm. It was a tight fit. Sure, there was room for a full-sized court but the space behind the base lines and the sides of the buildings was somewhat limited. Hence a deep smash was a sure winner.

Such a deep, hard smash executed by a strong arm used to steering a plough or ramming a fence post tight could create a problem. It felt good to the person who had just won the point, maybe a quiet 'bugger it' from the opponent whose toss was not good enough, but the ball would at times fly over the high wire-netting fence. Often the clean, white ball would land in a cow patty. Oh, crap! It would have to be retrieved before the game could be continued. Only two balls were used when playing in those frugal post World War II days.

Then it would have to be cleaned depending on the age of the cow manure. Were it old, a simple dusting off would suffice. A ball landing in a soft, fresh heap would require more attention.

On other occasions the smashed ball would land on the roof of the milking bails. This saved it from a messy landing in the cow yard, but someone would need to climb onto the roof to retrieve it. This job usually fell to one of us younger kids who were hanging around; especially if it was close to afternoon teatime. It was not an onerous task. Simply climb up a flimsy, home-made ladder which was permanently stationed there and throw the ball back onto the court usually past the player who wanted it, just to annoy him.

The height of the fence was not the problem. It was probably four metres high, tightly strung between iron-bark posts sourced from someone's forested hillside. It was then erected by farmers who knew how to erect good, strong fences, be it to keep the neighbour's bull out or a firmly driven forehand drive in. But not a winning smash!

Ours was an ant-bed court, fast and true when in good condition but the surface can deteriorate. Years of slipping and sliding by the players had taken its toll. I remember the court being resurfaced and upgraded with a new layer of ant-bed because the subsurface was beginning to show through. The players decided it should be fixed up during the off-season. This was summer. Tennis fixtures were played during the winter months. Cricket was the summer sport. The work would be done during a week when there was a lull in farm work.

On the nominated day, the regular players turned up with picks and shovels ready to start the job. The horses were yoked to the old German wagon and all set off up Frankie's hill to dig up and collect the hard anthill material. This was the closest location where there was an abundance of anthills sticking up through the grass. This material sets rock hard, and it is for this reason that they make a good playing surface. But it was hard work digging them up by hand and then loading the material on to the wagon to be taken down to the court. Remember that this was summer in South-east Queensland where the days are hot and muggy. Copious amounts of cold tea and water were needed to lubricate the hard work. Farmers were used to hard work and the whole exercise was seen as relaxation and a social outing.

Load after load was fetched until the piles were gauged to have sufficient material to get the job done. Then it had to be smashed up very finely, levelled, watered, levelled, allowed to set, then levelled again. This process went on for some weeks until the surface was hard, level and true. A new top-quality court emerged.

The members of the club, for it was a club affiliated with the Lockyer Valley Tennis Association (or whatever it was called) were all farmers who lived within a short distance of the court. They were a pretty fair bunch of players too. They would be up with the A grade competition winners more often than not. Tall strapping lads they were, who could hit a ball as hard as ramming in a fence post. But not only brute strength was used in their play. They also knew their way around the court and their rough, gnarled working hands could easily direct the racquet which they were holding to execute a delicate dropshot..

With courts like ours found everywhere there were many kids like me who had the opportunity of being introduced to tennis at a young age. I enjoyed playing tennis and took every opportunity available to practise my skills. My father, ever ready to advance my sporting abilities, had erected a practice board on the side of the dairy. His real reason for this, I suspect, was because I had begun playing in the dining room hitting the ball against the bathroom door. This continuous clunk, bang! Clunk, bang! echoed throughout the whole house. I was not popular.

'Stop that confounded noise. I'm trying to listen to the wireless.'

'Be careful, Son, Mum has some of her special China pieces on the sideboard there. You wouldn't want to mishit and break any.'

Now with my newly built wooden opponent waiting on the side of the dairy, I could take my racquet and a couple of balls and go out and practise to my heart's content: forehand, backhand, volleying, serving. That wall could accommodate my every wish and always send the balls speeding back to me. And I did become quite competent in the game and the sound of tennis balls bouncing in the dining room became a thing of the past.

20. Tennis Anyone?

Some of the kids with beginnings like mine went on to become champions and back then Australia became known worldwide as the land of tennis players. This brings to mind the time I spent in Germany a number of years later. 'You're from Australia, aren't you?' I was often greeted with words such as this (in actual fact they would have sounded more like: *Sie kommen aus Australien, gell?*). And then they would continue, 'You must be able to play tennis?'

'Yes, I do play,' I had to admit. This was when I was hitting the ball quite well.

'You must come and have a game.'

'Yes, that would be great, but I left my gear back in Australia.'

'So? We do have sports stores here in Germany, you know. Even here in Offenbach.'

'Well, I suppose . . .'

'Good, I will take you to the club for a game next Sunday.'

I bought a fashionable outfit – shorts, shirt, jumper (it does get cold in Germany) socks, shoes – which set me back quite a few Deutsch marks. Oh, and a racquet too. Why the special gear? You may ask. The tennis to which I was invited was at a special club. It was a kind of gentleman's club with tennis court attached. I played there a number of times but foolishly, I kept beating the local members. The number of invitations gradually dropped off.

When the court at home was being resurfaced, I was just a kid who hung about hitting tennis balls but still too young to be drafted into a competitive team. By the time I was old enough I was off to boarding school, played my tennis there and never became a real member of the club.

During the summer months that court doubled as a cricket

pitch for my mate Cecil and me. We were both keen schoolboy cricketers. We would often play a two-man cricket match on the court. I would bowl to Cecil until I got him out ten times. While batting he would score runs – one for hitting the fence behind the batting wickets, two for the off-side fence, three for the on-side fence and a four when the ball got through to the back fence. Over the fence was a six BUT also out. When his innings was finished, he would be the bowler and I the ten batsmen.

The years passed, one tennis season after the next – Saturday fixtures, afternoon teas, farmers' talk (the weather, price of crops, the weather, so-and-so's health, the weather). This was a social outing for all concerned but some keen competition as well.

The era of the country tennis competition gradually began to die. The club eventually was disbanded. Kikuyu grass took over the court and it became a good horse yard. Now even that has been disbanded and the area cannot be recognised as once being a smooth, fast, hard tennis court. Its glory days have long passed.

The team of winners I remember, Reg and Alex, Ron and Ronnie, have all passed away. I wonder do their children, or grandchildren or even great grandchildren know about the time when they were part of the do-it-yourself Tent Hill Tennis Club? They built their own court and their reputations by being hard workers and good country tennis players. They knew me as the kid who collected the balls out of the crap in the cow yard or threw them back off the roof of the cow bails.

21.
D.I.Y.

WERE ONE TO MENTION the words 'maul' and 'wedges' today, what if anything would spring to people's minds?

'You mean the one in the centre of the city?'

'That's a mall. Were you ever chosen for a spelling bee? No. That figures. I don't have that in mind for I'm talking about a maul.'

'Oh. A maul.' A rugby player's (or keen follower's) face starts to light up. 'It's a rugby term for when the chap with the ball is being torn apart by both the opposition and his own team members.'

Auch! And they call rugby a sport. You have to be really game to play it!

In terms of the official rules, 'a maul is formed when the ball carrier is held by one or more opponents or one or more of the ball carrier's teammates holds on (binds) as well (a maul therefore needs a minimum of three players). The ball must be off the ground.'

Clear? But then most agree that interpreting the rules of rugby union is a difficult task.

Reading that explanation, I can certainly see its semblance to being mauled by a lion, a most unfriendly lion at that, with its snatching and tearing, punching and shoving, hurting and injuring, roaring, shouting and cursing (well, perhaps not from a lion!).

I remember when I played rugby union many years ago that being involved in a maul was a most unpleasant experience. One could certainly question whether people play rugby for enjoyment. Luckily it rarely happened that I was involved in a maul, for as a wing/threequarters, I was well advised to keep away from forwards who seemed to have an appetite for that sort of violence. But inevitably there would be times when I ventured too close to those marauding packs, or was unable to move away quickly enough, and would be gathered up in one of those regulated tug-of-wars. I remember that at the time I completely disagreed with the coach's assessment that it was character building.

I still do. But I survived. Right now, I am not thinking about that type of maul. I've had enough of them!

And it's a wedge I want to refer to, not a wedgie. The wedges used on the farm when I was a kid could not be bought in a restaurant with steak and salad.

A restaurant? Going to a restaurant was something that just didn't happen when I was a kid. There was the odd occasion when father might slip into Peter's café for a bite to eat if the pig sale was running late and it was past his lunch time, i.e. twelve noon. That would be an emergency. Eating with friends and relatives was something you did at Sunday

21. D.I.Y.

lunch at home, not in a café in Gatton.

No, the maul and wedges were tools my dad used to make hardwood fence palings out of logs of wood. One was not able to go to Bunnings and pick up a load of ready-made palings. Bunnings didn't exist then, and if you wanted some palings you could either go to Hood's Sawmill in Gatton or make them yourself. Why pay for them? Make them yourself. This was the age of D.I.Y. I really do mean do it yourself, with the emphasis on the DO.

First of all, he (i.e. my dad as well, I could add, most farmers in the district) had to make the maul. This was a large, heavy, hammer-like tool. The head would consist of a round length of hardwood about a foot long with a diameter of six to eight inches cut from a solid log. Father would fashion steel rings of steel in his blacksmith's shed which he would then fit tightly around both ends of this piece of wood. This was to stop the wood splitting apart when used to hammer objects.

A long handle of about three feet was then fitted into this head to create a strong, heavy hammer – a maul.

And the wedges? He did not make these himself but got them from the local blacksmith over the hill at Ma Ma Creek. These were iron, wedge-shaped implements that looked like pieces cut out of a round cake. They would come in various sizes, sharp at one end and with a flat surface at the other end to hit with the maul.

Now armed with this maul, half a dozen wedges and a crosscut saw he would set about splitting palings from lengths of iron bark logs. And he also had his adze handy to strip off the splintery bits and so make them nice and smooth.

A pile of palings is a long way from a pig pen which father

was making. So he pressed on.

With crowbar and shovel he would dig holes in which to position the posts which he had previously cut from the forest. Once rammed tight with a rammer which he also had made himself, he would string wire between the posts. This was needed to hold the palings in place.

Yes, my dad was a do-it-yourself man, and not only for things required on the farm. He also enjoyed working with fine furniture timber, mainly silky oak which was readily available. When farm-work permitted he would be in his workshop working on one project or another.

'What ya doing Dad?' I asked as he was working on a piece of silky oak with his fretsaw.

'I'm shaping a leg for a plantstand I'm making for Mum.'

'Give me a go?'

'No, I don't think so. This is my last fretsaw blade.'

'I'll be careful this time.'

Father was always happy to pass on his skills to me, but the safety of his tools was a priority. His mildly spoken 'I don't think so' was really a definite no, so I did not pursue the matter. He smiled at me and continued sawing, carefully following the line he had drawn on the timber.

I was into this D.I.Y. stuff as well. In most cases it was a matter of had to be rather than chose to be. It was the only way of getting what I wanted in the way of toys. Shop shelves then were not awash with toys like they are today and parents, generally, weren't as anxious to waste money on them as they are today.

If I wanted a tractor for my miniature farm which I had created in the dirt under the house, I would make it using

21. D.I.Y.

a cotton reel and a rubber band. My farm was fenced with used match sticks and cotton from a drawer in Mum's sewing machine. The well was dug with a knife and spoon which I was careful to return to the kitchen without being seen. Coloured pebbles from the road made up the various animals. What would one expect living in the same house as my dad? I would follow in his footsteps and have a do-it-yourself farm.

My D.I.Y. did not stop there.

'I really came to make a boat.'

He stopped his sawing and looked at me. 'A boat?'

'Yes, a sailing boat. Not a real one but a toy one.'

'What put that idea into your head?'

'Clem's cousin, or someone, gave him one that really sails on their dam. I thought that I could make one that really sails too.'

'What, do it all by yourself?'

'Why not? Who would help me?'

'Hmm. Right! I can't see any real problem there. So how are you going to start?'

This was probably a good time to approach father with my idea of making a boat for he was keen to get on with what he was doing and not wanting to stop to point out to me all the problems which I might encounter. He also could keep an eye on me and give me a hand if needed.

'I need a piece of soft wood about so long,' as I held up my hands to the appropriate distance, 'that I can shape and hollow out like the South Sea Islanders.'

'There should be a suitable piece lying around somewhere. Look in that heap of off-cuts over there in the corner.'

After a little scratching around I held a suitable piece of four by two pine aloft.

'This should do.'

'But go careful with my chisels. Don't go chiseling into any nails.'

'No, Dad. There's none in this piece, that I can see.'

After many days with the hammer and chisels and no doubt a few blue fingernails when I missed the chisel and hit one of my fingers – all part of the learning experience – my boat was ready to be launched. It was not a simple dug-out canoe but a sleek sailing boat complete with a mast (a piece of father's doweling) and my white Sunday handkerchief as the sail.

It wasn't all smooth sailing as you might expect and I did meet with a few hick-ups along the way. I had shaped and chiseled out the main part of the boat – Clem told me it was called the hull – put in the mast and sail and went down to the dam to try it out. How excited I was to place it on the water, but with the least bit of wind it would roll over. No matter how often I tried, the same thing happened.

I was about to go back home disappointed when my brother, Ronnie, turned up.

'What are you doing down here at the dam by yourself?'

'I'm trying out my sailing boat which I've just made.'

'Oh. You made it? Let's see if it sails.'

'I have already tried it out,' I replied, not wanting to show him my failure.

'Have you really? Well, I haven't seen it sail. So put it on the water so I can see how it goes.'

I could stall no longer.

'OK. Here you are,' as I gently placed it on the still waters of the dam. But alas, as I expected. Along came a few ripples made by Ronnie to get the boat moving and over it went.

21. D.I.Y.

I was surprised that he didn't laugh and ridicule me.

'Show me a look at that thing' demanded my brother as he picked the boat up out of the water. 'No wonder it won't stand up. There's no keel.'

'No what?'

'No keel. You need a thin piece of wood along the bottom here that goes down into the water to give it some stability.' Ron seemed the complete expert on marine design.

'Oh,' I replied weakly, not really knowing what he was talking about.

He could see that I was out of my depth and in a moment of brotherly love and concern – which so often can be lacking between a teenager and his kid brother – he came back to father's workshop with me and showed me what had to be done.

Now with keel and rudder, which my brother also told me about, my *Sweet Swallow*, the name I had written on the side, was ready to conquer the dam and sail into family history.

A mild westerly wind was blowing, ideal condition to go sailing. It was clear that Clem was excited as I was when we took the boat to the other side of the dam. We selected a spot where there were no reeds, put it on the water and gave it a gentle shove away from the bank. The sail caught the wind and away it glided.

Success! What a beauty. Clem and I were jumping around in excitement. And I had made it all myself, with a little advice from my brother.

It was skimming across the dam when in the middle it suddenly stopped and tipped over.

'What the...?' exclaimed Clem.

'Oh, hell! I've just realised,' I said.

'Realised what?' Clem wanted to know.

'The keel must have got caught on the fence across the dam. It gets covered when the dam is full. I didn't think of that.'

And there in the middle of the dam my D.I.Y. sailboat lay wrecked until Ronnie agreed to swim out and get it. At that time, I was not a good swimmer – probably not a swimmer at all – and not permitted to go swimming in the dam. I had to rely on my brother. After drying it out, and with a new sail (my good, Sunday handkerchief was ruined by the smelly dam water) it was back to the dam.

My boat did sail again.

22.

Break-up Day

AHH! BREAK-UP DAY, THE last day of school for the year, a day that heralds the beginning of the long summer holidays, a day of laughter and tears. But that's putting it a bit dramatically. I remember seeing a lot of laughter on those days, and a lot of silliness, but tears? Maybe from one or two of the older girls who were leaving school for good, but I never actually saw any. And to be honest, if they felt tears coming, they would have gone behind the play-shed or into the girls' toilet. Girls just didn't cry in front of boys! No, it was a happy day.

For some (actually MOST back then) in grades seven and eight, this was the day they had been looking forward to all year. Finally, it was time when they were allowed (by law) to leave school. Had learnt everything that the school had to teach – or so we thought! It was time now to work full-time on the farm. Perhaps earn some money.

But what did it really mean for those kids – young teenagers – who were leaving school?

For some it would mean doing part-time jobs on the family farm, like bottle feeding and caring for the poddy calves, of which when sold you might get a part of the proceeds, depending on how things were going generally on the farm. Or you were left with those jobs your older brothers and sisters did not want to do: the dirty jobs like cleaning out the cow bails, washing the separator, keeping the pig troughs clean, chipping khaki prickles.

This position would then be passed down to the next in line when they left school and were eagerly awaiting the opportunity to earn a few bob.

For others it meant that now you were able to work on the farm as a man beside your dad (or as a woman beside your mum), doing real money-earning activities. You might even get paid a few quid for your work if that's the way your dad (the boss of the farm) wanted to arrange things. Perhaps you would be allotted a few acres on which you could grow your own crops, care for them and then finally reap the financial reward; assuming there was one. This was a kind of rural apprentice scheme, training to be a real farmer.

Or if there was no spot for you on the family farm, you could pick up a job somewhere in the local area. This might mean working on another farm which had run out of children, maybe in the local butter factory, perhaps an off-sider for one of the produce carters, or doing seasonal work like picking spuds and corn or cutting onions. There was usually something around. Staying on in the local area was preferable to having to leave home. So break-up day, as this last day of the school year was widely called, was important for those leaving school. Even so, no great deal was ever made of it. To the few going

22. Break-up Day

on to a secondary school somewhere it was merely the end of another school year.

I remember break up day as a sort of school picnic day; an alternative sports day, mainly because we didn't have a real sports day (athletic carnival) like some of the big schools. Our school was too small, besides which we all knew who could run the fastest or jump the longest. Coming first, or last, in a race of some sort would only show what everyone knew.

This day for us was filled with all sorts of novelty races being held on the schoolground. Most were organised by the parent group. This meant the mothers for most dads would find it difficult to take a day off during the week for a picnic, or so they said.

Looking back, I would have to say that we pupils were a very egalitarian group. Being the fastest runner, or the longest jumper, for example, didn't make one special. That was just who that person was. Charlie, to take an example, was not the fastest, but on the other hand he knew more swear words than anyone else. And Noel was a strong man (boy really). He could throw a bag of spuds onto the back of a truck while only in grade seven. No, Mr Barton didn't teach him that but was well aware of his capabilities and would summon Noel whenever something heavy had to be moved.

Everyone was accepted for what they were and what they weren't, for what they could do and for what they couldn't. Break-up day (the first day of the next school year really) saw the changing of the guard, for the positions of those leaving the school (assuming that they were the somethingest at school) would now be filled by someone else.

There would always be the strongest, the fastest, the

clumsiest, the tallest, the neatest writer, the smartest (at doing sums, or spelling, or whatever). This is what the different kids were. They were born with their special gifts and were accepted as such.

That is not to say that there was no competitive spirit within the school. There was always the least competitive pupil as well as the most competitive. Attend break up day and you will definitely see it on display. During my last couple of years at the school I was the fastest runner but I could not win the egg-and-spoon race, a feature event on this last school day of the year. Everyone else would try their best to beat me even, and I think I can rightly say this, by going to unsportsmanlike lengths to gain an advantage.

Yes, it appears that there was someone who could be called the unsportmanlikest pupil!

After these many years, I still feel that the egg-and-spoon race represented one of the frustrations of my school days. I could never win it although I believed that I should win it. The problem was, I see now, that I always approached the race too carefully. We had to supply our own egg from home, and I would leave for school with Mum's words clearly fixed in my mind: 'Now don't break it!'

During the race I would run at walking pace so that the egg would stay safely in the spoon. After all, an egg is an egg and once broken with its entrails scattered amongst the downtrodden grass it was of little use to anyone.

Only later did I realise that Mum meant I wasn't to break it on my way to school. During the race it was to take its chances. I thought that my natural speed, at walking pace, would win the day. How wrong I was. I underestimated the

22. Break-up Day

competitiveness and cunningness of the opposition.

Selly had a scientific approach to the event. He would boil his egg. The reason was no secret. That would stop the yoke bouncing and wobbling around with the movement of the arm and so provide stability. This didn't work out in practice for I can still see him sitting on the grass, halfway through the race, eating his boiled egg.

Then there was Noel. He would usually win. His egg remained firmly fixed in his porridge spoon even with his jerky running style. We all assumed that he was not playing fair and the word was that he had put honey on the bottom of his egg to stick it to the spoon. This was confirmed when we saw bees buzzing around him at the finishing line.

The chaff bag race was another which caused annual frustration for me.

One of the mothers would bring the chaff bags. They were used chaff bags, unlikely to be new for used ones were cheaper to buy and most farmers would have opted for these. Therein lay the problem for me in competing in this race. The race involved, as you all are probably aware (or maybe not), climbing into the empty bag, positioning your feet in the two bottom corners, pulling the top of the bag up as high as possible – probably up to one's chin – and then racing over a certain distance. This could be around thirty yards. I don't remember the exact distance, probably never did know for distance wasn't the important factor in the race. It was long enough for half the competitors to get their feet mixed up in a loosely held bag, fall head over heels and be left strewn along the racetrack.

My problem with this race was more medical than physical. The lucerne dust inside the second-hand chaff bags would quickly bring on my hay fever and bouts of sneezing. If I could jump into the bag immediately before the race was to begin and finish before the sneezing began, well and good. However if there was a holdup at the starting line, and my sneezing began, chaff-bagging to my potential became impossible.

It's just not possible, believe me, to run quickly in a bag and keep sneezing at the same time. In my case the dust would bring on not just one delicate achoo (Gesundheit!) but a vigourous bout, one violent explosion after the other.

Yes, the day was full of testing events, a veritable Upper Tent Hill Olympics. As well as the egg-and-spoon race and the chaff-bag race there was the three-legged race where you had to draw your partner out of the hat. I remember two years in a row – my last two years at the school – I drew out a couple of the shortest girls in the school for partners in the race. As I was fairly tall for my age ('an early grower', Mum would tell everyone) coordinating our steps, and hence any chance of winning was difficult, nigh impossible. Yes, completely impossible.

The piggyback race was another race where one's partner

22. Break-up Day

(the one you had to carry on your back) was drawn out of the hat. I must point out that most kids at the school were lean creatures, having spent so much time running around the hillsides of the district. There were a couple of names that brought forth a 'Oh hell. No!' when drawn out.

I remember teaming up with Noel for the wheelbarrow race at his last year at school. I got to hold his legs (the handles) and he would run along in front of me on his two strong arms (the wheel). All was going well until near the end when Dessie and Clem caught up and we were in danger of being beaten. I upped the speed but Noel's tired arms couldn't respond and collapsed. I drove Noel's face into mother earth. There were parents present, mainly mothers, and what Noel said couldn't be heard by everyone (luckily). Those near us agreed that he could challenge Charlie as the best swearer in the school.

All these races were great for us sporty types, but the highlight of the day was not seen out on the school yard but in the shelter of the play-shed. Here stood a couple of green, canvass cylinders. We all knew, from previous experience, what was inside them: dry ice keeping small tubs of ice-cream from melting. On a call from one of the mothers all the pupils would line up to be given their small tub of ice-cream and a wooden spoon. Well not really a spoon but a small piece of wood which could be used as a spoon.

This was a treat which seemed to make the year at school worthwhile.

www.ingramcontent.com/pod-product-compliance
Lightning Source LLC
Chambersburg PA
CBHW031243290426
44109CB00012B/410